EP Sport Series

All about Judo
Badminton
Basketball
Competitive Swimming
Conditioning for Sport
Cricket
Field Athletics
Football
Golf
Hockey for Men and Women
Improve Your Riding
Learning to Swim
Men's Gymnastics
Modern Riding
Netball
Rock Climbing
Sailing
Snooker
Squash Rackets
Start Motor Cruising
Table Tennis
Tennis up to Tournament Standard
Track Athletics
Trials Bike Riding
Underwater Swimming
Volleyball
Wildwater Canoeing
Windsurfing
Women's Gymnastics

EP PUBLISHING LIMITED
1978

P

ep sport

orienteering

m henley

To my wife, Mina, and Brian, Nicola and Joanne

ISBN 07158 0591 6 (Hard)
ISBN 0 7158 0639 4 (Limp)

Published 1976 by EP Publishing Ltd, East Ardsley, Wakefield, West Yorkshire

Reprinted 1978
Reprinted 1980

Acknowledgements

Thanks are due to Graham Relf for various photographs and to Bob Wilson for developing prints far into the night.

Printed in Great Britain by G. Beard & Son Ltd, Brighton

CONTENTS

The Challenge of Orienteering

Most people think they can navigate, and no doubt they can, but can they do it well enough under competitive conditions? Are they able to unravel the puzzles set up by the course planner and then chase and follow the best route? If the shortest distance between two points on a map is a straight line, is it always the quickest route on the ground? Why does the careful and methodical orienteer manage to beat the extremely fit and fast orienteer sometimes? This book will provide some of the answers, and introduce this fast-growing sport to the whole family, who can either take it seriously or simply enjoy competing. It is one of the few sports that caters for all ages and abilities. There is always the challenge that your knowledge of navigation and finding your way using a detailed map might not be up to the standard of the planner. The aim is for all competitors to

All ages

enjoy the course while pitting their wits against his. Thus to find each control is a pleasure and to complete the entire course is very satisfying. Nobody really minds if you walk or run, but the more you succeed, the more you will wish to take up the challenge and cut your times to a minimum, to beat your friends and relatives.

Beware—once hooked, it is a sport you can't give up!

Final sprint for home—note streamers on trees leading to finish ▶

Red deer stag

Perhaps you are one of those people who say they have never seen a deer, in which case that is another reason why you should take up this sport. Orienteering is the ideal sport for actually tripping over one! You may not be familiar with the countryside and the forests, but time spent orienteering will soon alter that. You may be one of the millions who live in large towns and are unable to head for the hills very often.

However much you like your own town you must dislike scenes like this.

Pollution

Serious compass work

Perhaps you are missing too much.

Well, suppose you were suddenly whisked off into a beautiful forest, could you find your way about? If you had a map, you might say—but remember most people who think they can map-read are all right on tracks but quite out of their depth when they leave the beaten track!

Now what's it all about?

Essentially the winner is the fastest navigator round a varying number of points in the forest. The competitor only learns of the exact locations a few moments after his start time, and then has to reach them all in sequence in as short a time as possible. Competitors in a championship event need to run as fast as they can over the whole course as literally every second counts. The course may be 9 or 10 miles for seniors, but the final total times are often separated by only a few seconds.

Ordinary Events cater for people from age 10 to 60 plus and each course is designed to meet the capabilities of each age group.

Often, many novices alternate running and walking but nobody will ever complain for it is up to each individual to enjoy himself, so do not worry about your own initial fitness. Courses may be 1, 2 or 3 miles for novices.

The Wayfarers Course is for absolute novices and youngsters without the confidence to travel far into the forest. This may also be the course available to mother and the pushchair, and will therefore keep to large tracks, avoiding hills and difficult features.

A control here would be 'On the Path' ▶

Orienteering—the family sport

The orienteering season in Britain tends to start in about September and end in June, although these days there is often no close season at all and as many as five or six events may be staged simultaneously throughout Britain on some weekends. There is now a rapidly increasing following which is very encouraging considering that the sport was only started in Scotland in 1962 by the founding of the Scottish Orienteering Association. This was followed in 1965 by the English Orienteering Association, and finally, in 1967 the British Orienteering Federation was set up. The international body is known as the I.O.F.—International Orienteering Federation.

Events Held

Club Events

Road and ride junction ▶

These may only have about 30 or 40 competitors. The map may be fairly rough and the organisation is informal and may just be done by two or three enthusiasts.

Tapes to finish. Gap in wall will be shown on the map
▼

This man would be disqualified as only full arm and leg cover is allowed ▶

Expert orienteers

Badge Event

This would be an efficient large event with perhaps 200–500 runners from all over the country.

All the organisation, map making, course setting and officiating is checked by a very experienced orienteer. He is called the controller and has the overall responsibility of making sure that everything is correct.

The name, badge event, refers to the fact that a National Scheme is in operation for the award of badges. These are based on the competitors' performance compared to the winner's time. The easiest badge is iron, then bronze, silver and finally the coveted gold badge—everyone is eligible and all they have to do is to succeed in events designated badge events.
(See page 88 for details.)

Waiting for friends

The J.K.

Starting lines

A massed start

The large results ladder

Championships

There are District Championships, followed by Regional Championships, such as the Scottish, and finally the British Championships. At the higher levels teams are picked and indeed a constant record of performances is kept to find the best international team.

The highlight of the year in Britain is usually the memorial event to Jan Kjellstrom, the son of the Swedish manufacturer of Silva Compasses, who was killed in a car crash. He did a tremendous amount of work to get the British interested in orienteering and for enjoyment this event should not be missed.

There are usually over 1,000 competitors, including orienteers from Norway, Sweden, Denmark, France, Germany and other European nations. The event occurs at Easter and is spread over four days. A warm-up event is followed by the Individual Championship race and on the third day a Relay event takes place.

Finally, the competition has a finishing-off fourth day. In the evening there is always a Social or Dance and the international rivalry and friendliness is tremendous.

Types of Event

World Championships

These occur biennially in September. The Scandinavians usually dominate this scene which is not really surprising since they invented the sport and it is usually a compulsory sport at all of their schools. British orienteers are beginning to appear quite high up the results, but who knows, you could be a future British Champion and the first Briton to win the World Championships.

Cross-country Orienteering

The most common contest will take place over forest, moorland or fields in the form of a single course. It could be a winding trail from the start and finish elsewhere but normally the planner aims to get a circle so that the finish is near the start. This allows for the re-use of helpers and avoids the problem of taking the runners' belongings to the finish.
After you cross the start line, you visit the master maps to copy down your course and then you will have to find about a dozen control markers. A control is simply a point in the forest which is mapped; any recognisable feature might be used but there are rules about the description of the point. A paper called a description sheet is issued to tell you what you are looking for. It might say 'The path bend', 'the ditch junction', 'the re-entrant', 'the depression',

The planner is setting up a control marker

etc. Your map, when copied from the master map, will show the points as red circles. The object you are seeking is located exactly at the centre of the circle but it is not marked with a dot. In cases where several similar features are clustered together, if difficulties might occur, then the description of the control will be, for example, 'Northernmost depression'. In the forest a control marker is hung in the **exact** position; this is checked by pacing and compass bearings. It is a flag really but its shape is that of a hollow prism of triangular section. The sides are diagonally divided, to show the bottom half Orange Red at the bottom and the top half White. On it or near it, will be a notice with a code letter or number; it is essential that you cross-check this with the code on your description sheet. It will never be wrong, so if it does not match you are at the wrong control.

Sometimes controls may be put on features which are also being used for other courses, but, if there were two knolls widely separated then one might be an M15 control, code 'Z', and the other, an M21, might be code 'R'. This means the first would be meant for 15-year-olds, the second for 21-year-olds. Woe betide you if you mark the wrong one, you will be disqualified when you reach the finish. To prove you have visited the site there is always a method of marking your control card. Thus Control 2 will have a clipper or a punch with perhaps a diamond shape, and this will be cut into the Control 2 box on your control card. The correct marks must be in the correct sequence for the cards to be checked back at the finish. If you forget to clip your card, even once, you will be disqualified.

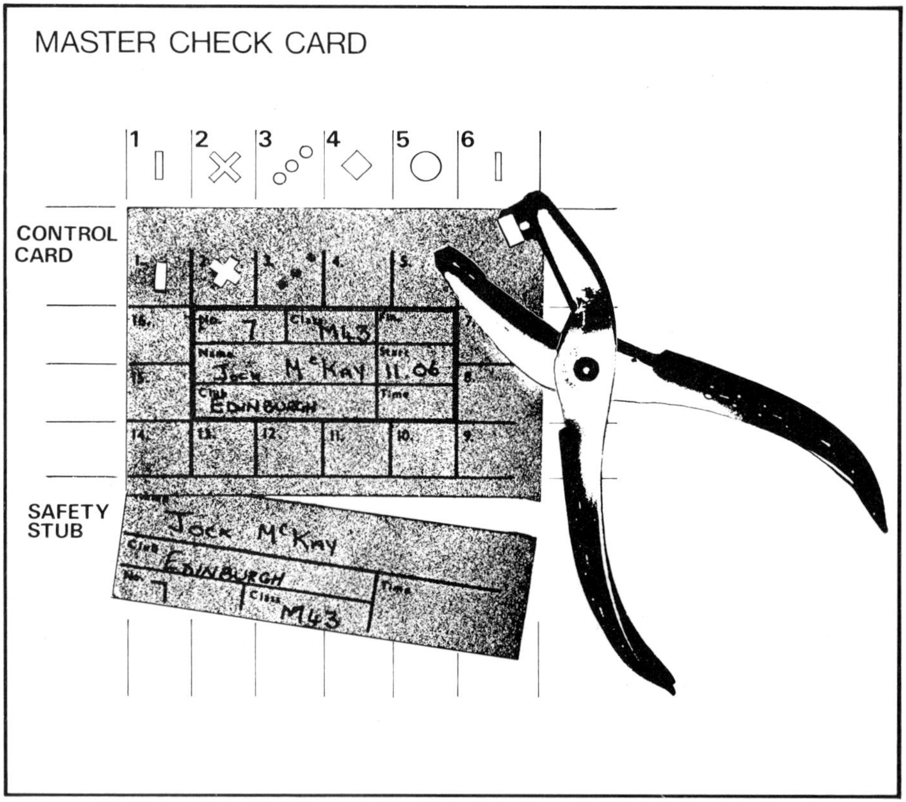

To summarise, if there are 12 controls you must visit them in the correct sequence and you must check the code letter and stamp or clip your control card in the correct position. You must find all the 12 controls and finish the course to be included in the results.

Score Event

If you know what to expect in this competition you can have a lot of fun. When you arrive for your start-time, you will be given a map with up to 40 or 50 Red circles overprinted on it to indicate the controls that have been placed in the forest. Your job is to visit as many as possible in the allotted time, which is usually an hour or 90 minutes. Also overprinted will be the values; the farther or more difficult controls have a high value such as 30 points, but easy and close controls may be worth only 5 or 10 points. You may only be able to reach about 15 or 20 of these features and may score a total of perhaps 230 points. Therefore, it is essential to work out the course you choose before you start, so that you can take in as many of the high-scoring places as possible. If you are late back to the finish there is a penalty score of five points per minute, which is subtracted from your total. Five minutes late would thus be 25 off, equivalent to about two hard-earned controls and lateness is therefore definitely to be avoided.

▲ The Crag Foot, showing a mass start

They're off

Sometimes everybody will start a score event at the same time—this is known as a Mass Start—but you must be prepared for your own choice of routes with no thought of following the herd.

This type of start might also be used for a relay race with all the teams sending off their first 'leg' at the same time. International Teams may compete over a type of cross-country course which involves a different stretch for each member of the team. This either means that each member returns to the same start point or, if there is sufficient organisation, it would mean that each member of the team starts from separate areas. This can be tremendous fun and you soon make friends in this sort of event, so don't refuse an invitation to make up a team.

Night Event

This must be experienced to be believed; anyone who says navigating at night is easy has obviously not tried it. Golf courses are excellent with their hills and bunkers and rough and bushes.

Sand dune areas too are admirable for this type of event. However, even the most straightforward public park becomes difficult for night orienteering. Every flower bed, bank, strip of trees or bushes, bandstand or fountain becomes a mystery to be carefully negotiated on an accurately paced compass bearing. Even if you are familiar with the area by day you may be hard pressed to complete the course in the dark.

Don't waste your time by turning up without a torch, it's impossible. The best sort of light is fixed to the head or the coat to leave the hands free for compass and map work. You will not travel far or fast so wrap up warm. The more timid girls might feel happier in twos in the dark. It is very odd to see a row of lights bobbing about in a business-like way obviously on the same trail; this event is a must for the keen orienteer.

Street Event

This is a useful variation for a training session and ingenious courses can be set to provide a lot of fun.

Orienteering and Other Sports

Variations on conventional orienteering can be easily organised, but other sporting enthusiasts can also adopt this sport for a novelty event within their own annual programme. If you are a horse rider, why not suggest an orienteering competition on horseback? This will need an orienteer and a horseman to combine in the organisation to ensure the

Orienteering on wheels

Orienteering afloat

feasibility of the routes available. Aquatic orienteering is another possibility if the right area is available, so if you are in Canoe or Sailing Clubs you too might try an orienteering alternative for a summer club night. Remember it brings home to the members the importance of navigation and accurate compass bearings.

Hill walkers and mountaineering clubs might like to test new members in an orienteering contest before letting them on the hills. Many people are often too embarrassed to admit to not being perfectly confident in compass work, especially older well-established members.

Orienteering on horseback

Terrain

The types of terrain found in Britain are ideal for orienteering because of their beautiful and rugged scenery. There are thousands of acres of forest and even a small area can swallow up hundreds of people without them disturbing each other. The coniferous woods have such close foliage that they are ideal for concealing small features such as knolls, ruins, large boulders, depressions, streams, paths, fences and old walls. These objects make excellent control points deep inside the forest, and since most tree-covered slopes look similar the orienteer has to be really on his toes to keep track of his exact position.

Moorland is excellent too, especially if it is adjacent to wooded areas. Patches of gorse and heather, lack of buildings and tracks, small marshes and ditches and the undulating, almost

▲
The summit is at the right. Note vegetation change in the valley

Our magazines

monotonous similarity in every direction contribute to the problems of navigation that can be posed.

SAND DUNES, particularly the giant variety, with plenty of grassy tussocks scattered about, also make excellent scenic competition areas. Each dune looks like the next and each depression has a definite stereotype nature. There are few helpful paths or definite boundaries, usually no streams and a complete absence of roads and habitation.

GOLF COURSES, especially seaside links, are equally as good with their artificial mounds, depressions and sand bunkers in all directions. The greens and bunkers are out of bounds, of course, but that leaves water traps, awkward copses and doglegs to navigate around!

Your First Contact

Take up the sport by making written or verbal contact with your nearest orienteering group. Try asking at schools or libraries for the secretary's address as this move is **essential** to obtain a list of the fixtures, which will be well scattered over the country. For information, write to The British Orienteering Federation, Lea Green, Nr. Matlock, Derbyshire DE4 5GJ. The clash with Saturday football, hockey or shopping has made orienteering a Sunday sport, but Churchgoers are usually able to accommodate both service and recreation in the one day. It has been proved, however, that support is drastically curtailed when events are held on Saturdays, as many schoolchildren have morning jobs if they are not actually involved in other sports. The fixtures list for Britain is always issued in the bi-monthly magazine called 'The Orienteer' or in 'The Scottish Orienteer'.

Do note the details for it may be a long way to travel to find entries have closed or you are not eligible. Please, in every case, try to enter in advance by post; it helps the organiser tremendously by allowing him to get your competition card ready instead of you queuing for it on the day.

Always enclose two stamped addressed envelopes with your entry; one for details and your control card, and the other for final results after the event. NOTE the region code for your area of Britain, S for Scotland, NW for North-West England and so on. When you have noted these, look and see what local club and training fixtures are being organised near you.
If you have nobody to travel with then go alone by whatever method

is convenient; once you join a local club you can share transport.

Fees are essential to cover the cost of the special 'O' maps, forest permits and parking facilities. They are very reasonable, even for large competitions which may well have 500 people entering the forest during the whole day, and the fees are reduced for Juniors. Club events, which are usually much smaller affairs, charge even more modest fees. Refreshments such as orange juice are usually free at the finish for competitors, but bring your own lunch unless the pre-event details say that food will be available.

Age Groups

Men	*Years*	
Older Veterans	50 +	M50
Veterans	43 +	M43
Senior Men	35 +	M35
Men	21 +	M21
Intermediates	19-20	M19
Young Men	17-18	M17
Junior Men	15-16	M15
Boys	13-14	M13
Young Boys	12 and under	M12

Women	*Years*	
Older Veterans	50 +	W50
Veterans	43 +	W43
Senior Women	35 +	W35
Women	19 +	W19
Young Women	17-18	W17
Junior Women	15-16	W15
Girls	13-14	W13
Young Girls	12 and under	W12

Make sure of your competitive age group before you go to a competition so that you can register for the proper course.

Prior to this you should gain experience on a wayfarers course or easy short course. This is strongly recommended for all age groups.

January 1 is always the reference point, so if you have had your 15th birthday you would, in the case of a boy, be in the M15 class. A lady of 34, with a birthday in, say April, would be in W35 after the following January 1. A club leader should register his team members to save long queues, in which case he will need to have each member's class, so make sure you know your own.

Whatever your age or ability, you should not hesitate to enter, you can always travel at your own pace and the distance will be a suitable length for you. Soon you will begin to meet people and recognise them or their name on each competition results board. A rivalry is certain to crop up and add a further spur to improvement of your own performance. Since competitors in the same class cannot start at the same time it is easy to find out if your rival is starting maybe 5 minutes ahead or 10 minutes behind you. In either case if you see him it is liable to increase your pulse rate! Members from the same club should be separated by 4 minute intervals according to the rules to prevent any following or advantage.

Clothes

When you start, wear an old sweater and jeans, with an anorak or waterproof for poor weather. Arms and legs must be fully covered at all times of the year. In winter, dress for the worst; rain and snow are likely and this should not deter orienteers. Although unlikely, remember that if you are lost or injured you do not want to risk exposure (severe chilling of the body), whilst help is on its way.

You can wear anything strong on your feet, such as walking boots or football boots. Gym shoes will do, but often slip off or tear, and do not grip the undergrowth; best of all are studded running shoes—not spiked ones. The older

Some wayfarers try the sport

generation may just want to wear old gardening clothes—if you do, don't worry, you won't be the only one! Ideally, you should make sure you have a good frontal pocket, such as some anoraks which have zips, for holding your whistle, and the biro and compass when not in use. They are practically guaranteed to get lost from ordinary trouser pockets and when in use make sure they are attached to the wrist for safety.
When you are convinced that you like orienteering, why not get an 'O' suit? This is made of light snag-proof nylon. It looks like a tracksuit but is made of material like a thin raincoat. An extra pocket is advisable with a flap secured by 'velcro' rather than a zip or buttons. This will hold your description sheet and control card if so desired. **'O' shoes** are really studded running shoes made of some non-absorbent material such as PVC or rubber, but not leather. They will need to be sturdy to resist sharp sticks, boulders and undergrowth. Studs will be essential for grassy slopes, jumping from side to side of ditches, crossing old slopes of bracken, running on moss, heather and fresh pine needles.
Some people wear some sort of cap to stop pine needles or twigs from scratching the face, and to protect the eyes. It also prevents a collection of twigs or vegetation in the hair and some top orienteers also wear sweatbands. They find that perspiration on the forehead interferes with vision, and also sweaty hands tend to spoil the map, so they try to eliminate these annoyances with absorbent bands on the forehead and wrists.

Full 'O' suit and 'O' gear

Equipment

You should have a whistle, a compass, and a reliable biro—preferably red—when you arrive at a competition. Some people prefer a waterproof Chinagraph pen to a biro, especially if the map is covered. Red is preferable for copying your course at the master maps as it does not correspond with any of the coloured signs already present.
The protractor compass should be of the type made by Silva of Sweden or Suunto of Finland. The cheapest type will do while you are a novice, but make sure it has a short wrist cord so that you don't lose it if you fall over. The whistle should be loud and is for use **only in emergency**.
Useful additions to your equipment would be safety pins and polythene bags; their use will be described in detail later to keep your map, control card and control description sheet dry.

The Silva compass

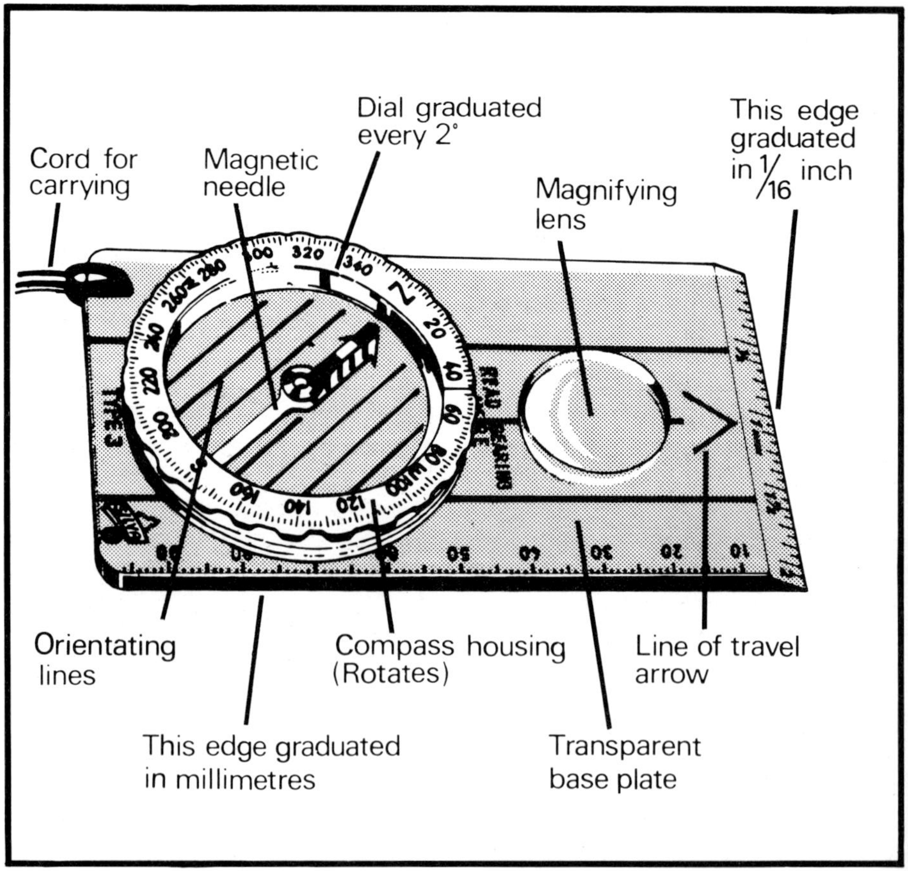

Procedure

Now let us examine briefly what to expect when you arrive at an event in the forest.

Try to be aware of the procedure when you first go to an event, but if in doubt any orienteer will be pleased to help.

Registration

This will be the place to look for to sign in your arrival if you have already entered by post, and you will be given your control card.

Sometimes late entries can be arranged on the day but please try to avoid this nuisance by pre-entry unless it is stated 'entry on the day only'.

Control cards and control description sheets

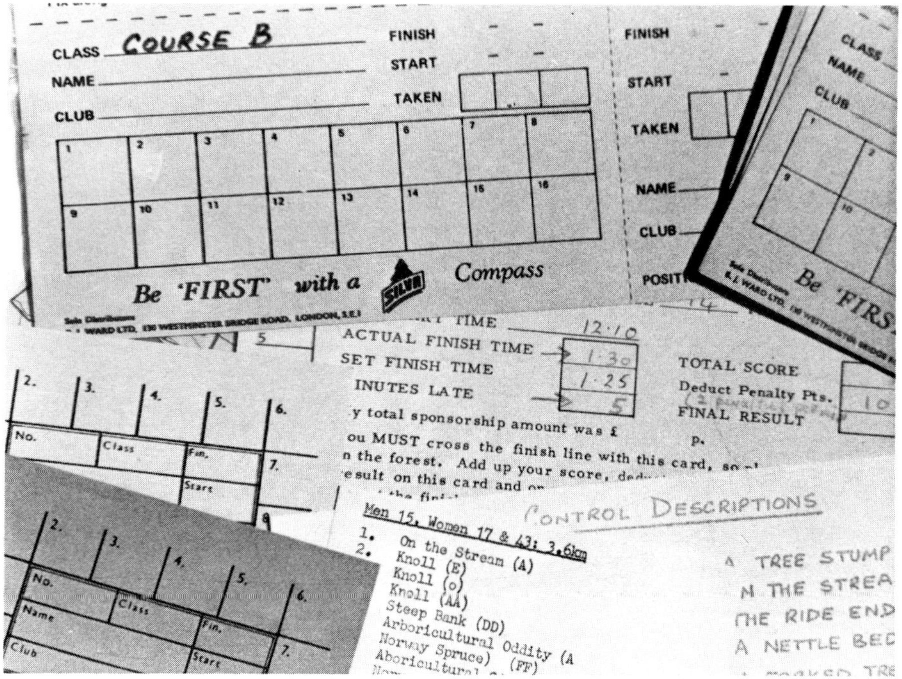

The official will need to check your name and club and particularly your age group on a card called a **control card**, which either you or the official will fill in. Note the tear-off section and ensure that your name, age group, and club are duplicated on it, at the top and bottom of the card.

As the start is staggered, you will find that you have been allocated a start time; make sure it is suitable for you and that you have enough time to change and

Registration

get to the start which may be several hundred yards away inside the forest. If you arrive late, it may be changed or the lateness will simply be time counted against your total time score. If you entered your name with the entry fee by post, you will have had advance warning of your start time. In this case, aim to arrive about an hour before that time.

You have perhaps 30 minutes to kill and will be milling about with competitors of all ages, but you must not enter the forest yet. Use the time to prepare well. Practise compass use and pace judgement and get yourself mentally attuned.

Remember that you will have to carry your description sheet and map as well as your control card. They could all go into your safety pocket, but might get all mixed up if you are not careful. So to sort things out, get a safety pin and pin your control card to your chest, forearm or waist. Use the locking pins meant for babies' nappies for your own protection! Make sure the card can be clipped without having to be removed from your clothes and without the need for acrobatics. It's a good idea to cover your control card on both sides to keep out moisture, rain, drizzle and perspiration. You can use a polythene bag, or a stiff map case, or if you want to jump into the ranks of the experts, go to a printer or stationer and buy some polythene with a sticky backing known as 'Transpaseal'.

Ten minutes before your start time move up towards the starting area.

Prestart

The first official will call out either your name or more likely your start time. It is your job to find out what race time is and to synchronise your own watch if you have one.
An event starts when it is ready, if it is due to start at 10 a.m. G.M.T. and is delayed 10 minutes all that is done is that the official clocks are altered; thus if your start time is 10.41 it means race time, **not** actual correct G.M.T. You can usually find race time on a clock at Prestart, or a number board, or it is being called out by the starter.

Anyway, make sure that you will move through the Prestart to arrive at the starter at your own exact start time.

Move into the first enclosure which may say MINUS 4 minutes.

Check that it is 4 minutes from your start time by finding out what the starter is shouting. Let us say you are due off at 10.41, then the 'race time' must be 10.37 when you step into the first box marked MINUS 4. If you are a minute later then adjust which enclosure you are in so that your start time will be correct.

Prestart among the ruins. Note competitors spread at minute intervals

In the photographs, watch that chap with the white tracksuit top. He has already registered his arrival at the event and has been given a start time of 12.06 and now the time is 11.56 and together with other competitors in different age groups he is waiting, no doubt anxiously, for his name to be called. He has not got his map or description sheet yet, so perhaps the best thing to do is to get his mind working on compass bearings or to jog-trot as a warm-up. At 12.01 on the time indicator board, his name is called by the official at the beginning of the Prestart boxed area. At Registration the time of removal of the controls was indicated on the notice board. This might also have shown other announcements or map corrections, such as out of bounds areas, or newly felled parts of the forest. When 12.01 was called he and the other runners in classes M17, M15, W13, M43, etc., moved forward into the first

Waiting for his name to be called ▼

The official calls out start times ▼

◀ Controls removed at 2.30

◀ 12.01 on the time indicator board

Forward into the first roped enclosure

The next roped-off enclosure

The final check of equipment

roped off area. You can see a tent in the photograph; this is a great asset at prestart for the distribution of maps, in case it is windy or raining. Each time the whistle blows, at one minute intervals, all the groups of runners move up one more roped enclosure. At minus 3 minutes a man can be seen asking for whistles to be shown. This is obligatory in competitions, particularly where forests are so extensive that in the winter exposure has to be contended with if a competitor is lost. No whistle—no start. You will also be checked for proper clothing, that is, full arm and leg cover, not shorts.

About 2 minutes before the start, one official will take your control card 'stub' as a receipt to show that you are in the forest. This is of tremendous importance for your safety, so make sure your stub is taken. All of the stubs are taken immediately to the finish so that they can be ticked off as each competitor returns. IT IS THEREFORE ESSENTIAL THAT ALL COMPETITORS REPORT TO THE FINISH, even if they give up, retire, get fed up or get a lift back. The organiser can only assume an accident has occurred if he is left with one or two stubs at the end of the day. He will then initiate a search, followed by a call to the Police, and he will get in the Mountain Rescue if necessary. So if you fail to report in and a search is initiated you can guarantee that your name will be totally blacklisted for several future events.

This is also the point where you will most likely receive your blank map and description sheet, so use the time to orientate yourself and the map before the actual start. You may have been given it before but not allowed to study it until now. If you have time, copy the description sheet onto your control card, then put the list carefully into another pocket out of the way.

When the starter blows his whistle and calls 12.06, you and others in **different** age groups are into actual race time; the clock is ticking against you, and every second counts.

You will now follow the tapes to the area called 'MASTER MAPS' and there you will look for the map with your age group marked on it. Perhaps you are in M15 group or M12. Copy your course down absolutely **perfectly**—one slip here and you will be looking for something which is not there.

▲
Follow the tapes to the master maps shown by a triangle on the map

◀ Map corrections

Master Maps

A master map is shown on p. 119. In some competitions the control points for each age group are overprinted onto the maps which are then given to you at the very last moment. They are printed as red circles of half a centimetre diameter—the very centre of the circle indicates the exact position of the control. There is no dot printed at the centre and if there were several small features such as large boulders shown, you would have to gauge the one at the middle as the indicated feature but your control description should give a precise definition and so help identify the feature.

The Boulder
(SE most)

In the majority of events, this is not done for reasons of expense and additional prior planning. You will therefore have to copy your own circles round each control point. Red biro is found to be most easily seen on the map. Remember to be very sure that you have circled the map with the **exact** location of the control at the centre of the circle to avoid being confused by duplicate features.

You will need your map at hand for the whole time so it will be better kept dry—there's nothing like a soggy map for getting yourself lost. Cover it as described previously.

Your job is now to visit all of your points in the correct order as fast as possible and then reach the finish. Obviously, therefore, it is important to copy from the master map very quickly as well as very accurately.

Experienced orienteers even practise this, by working out their own sequence of operations, perhaps going across or up and down on the map to find the features. This will be up to your personal preference. You will probably do the obvious thing and begin at 'start' and follow round copying the route until the 'finish'.

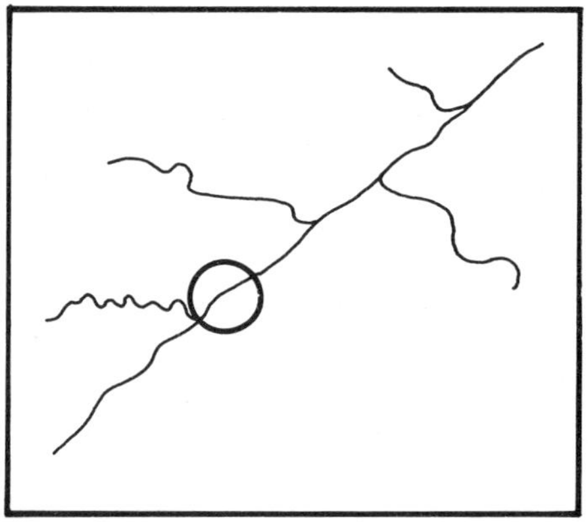

▲ 'On the Stream'

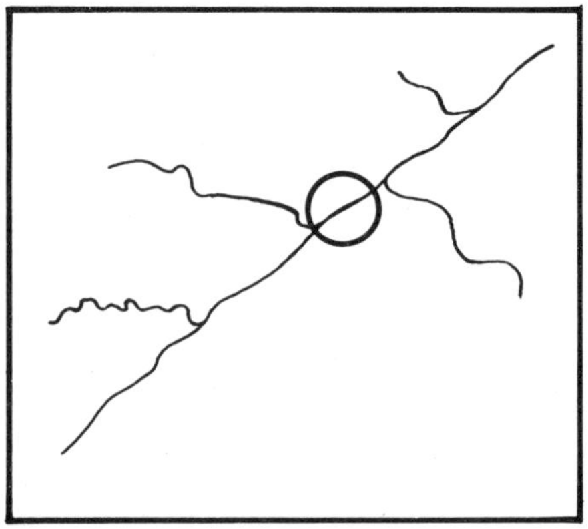

▲ Mistake

See map, p. 119.

Realise that the red triangle indicates EXACTLY the position of the master maps at its centre. May I suggest you also copy the numbers of the controls in proper sequence and include the straight lines between controls to give you a general impression of the shape or pattern of the whole route. This probably helps when you are tired and prevents you from missing out a control.

The FINISH line is always placed EXACTLY at the centre of the two concentric red circles on the map.

So don't leave it out just because there is not a control to be found. Nearly always there are tapes running part of the way from the last control to the finish, so that runners can have a final sprint home to use up their last energy or to give a measure of competitiveness to people finishing at the same time.

On long Senior Courses they sometimes employ split master maps. This could mean getting the first seven controls at the start and the second half of your course near the seventh control. It will be a simple board with a second master map pinned to it, on occasions it may also be manned as a check point.

As soon as you are sure you have copied everything accurately, set off for the first control.

The Brownmuir Map (p. 116) shows you what to expect at the Master map area shown by the red triangle. This course is the type given to schoolchildren or novices and you need to copy it exactly on to your blank map and visit all the 12 controls in the proper sequence. The route from the last control to the finish line will be marked with tapes, so use them for a final sprint home to save seconds.

Race to the finish tape

Reading the second master map

The description sheet for this course is (refer to p. 116):

1. The stream/ditch junction
2. The boulder
3. The small crag
4. The boulder
5. The depression (westernmost)
6. The lone tree
7. The boulder (easternmost)
8. The well (westernmost)
9. The depression
10. The ruin (S.E. Corner)
11. The depression
12. Junction of paths

Follow tapes to finish.

Gully or stream

The Course and the Setter

Let's see what happens to you as a novice when you try the wayfarers course. All orienteering should start this way. But how does one orienteer. Let's learn more about orienteering courses and techniques.

In a large competition the organiser will ask an experienced orienteer if he would like to set the courses for an event in perhaps 10 or 12 months' time. It needs to be as long as this to assess the area in the same season of the year.

A feasible late winter path may well be overgrown by brambles or ferns by autumn. In this case, let us assume the 'O' map is already available and has probably been used in previous competitions.

The Setter's prime objective is to make sure you enjoy the competition. He wants to test your

'On the fence'

map reading skill and your ability to navigate through various terrains to the utmost. Secondly, he wants to take you through the most interesting parts of the forest. You would soon take up something else if he dragged you on hands and knees through the thickest, dirtiest, prickly steep parts all the time.

Let us put ourselves in his position to see how he can do this, keeping those two objectives in mind. The Setter is not allowed to hide the control markers—they must be clearly visible from all directions from about 15 m. If one is not, then additional streamers must be put up near the control.

However, he can pose various problems which may lead you into trouble if you do not look very carefully before you decide on a route. So you have to think like the Setter and try to anticipate his plans. Look at the map on p. 114.

The setter had to choose a start near the road and placed it at A on Bar Hill. Since he wants the runners to go to 'the outcrop' at B he is probably trying to test their accuracy because, if you look closely at the map, there are six small rock outcrops close together in the thickly wooded area at B. The orienteers must be extremely

◀ Difficult scree slope beyond the runner. Control 'on the summit'

careful as soon as they cross the track because valuable minutes might be lost if they navigate to the wrong outcrop.

To find 'the boulder' at C, the Setter is demanding observant map reading, as a straight bearing from B is not good enough. A runner may seek out the small bank or that ditch that passes close to C. From the right-angle bend of the earth bank a quick compass check would lead into the correct boulder.

Now the course should bring them back into the forest so D is chosen as 'on the ditch'. Care is rewarded as it is the fifth ditch that must be entered among all the dense undergrowth.

Try to gain a fair idea of why the Setter has chosen that particular location for a control.

On the numbered example (1–2–3) the setter has made the direct route look attractive but is it? To find Control 1 surely you would avoid that boulder field, the crag and the steep summit. Then go to the right of it skirting the forest until you get to the track and that will save you a lot of wasted energy. To find Control 2 which is in runnable forest you have several choices apart from direct. Why not follow the ruined wall and up the ditch—it should be easy.

Now to find Control 3 which is the 'ditch end'. You could go straight to it via the woods but until you are happy about that technique you could follow the field boundary and the edge of the trees. In this way you will build up your confidence and familiarity with map reading.

Note large knoll inside forest boundary. Some beginners compare notes

In the Forest—Etiquette

As soon as you leave the master maps it is, of course, your job to visit all of the control points on your course in the correct sequence. The competitor with the shortest time is the winner, so the fitter you are the better. However, nobody will mind in the least if you are a casual competitor who likes a bit of a walk up the steep bits. You may be in one of the more senior age groups and I assure you the prime object is for you to enjoy the cunning problems of navigation and to lead you to the more beautiful parts of the forest. The hares and tortoises choose their own routes and pace and this is why orienteering is such an admirable family sport. Father and Son each have their own length of course and if Mother and Daughter are also inclined towards the sport there

Clipping your card with a needle punch at the control

will be a course appropriate to each of their abilities.
The competitor must not follow other people under the rules of the sport. This would be foolish anyway since you have no way of knowing if others are on the same course as you. However, you should adopt a small amount of evasion in case you are followed. If you have just found a difficult control you must avoid leading everyone to it for they will save seconds to their own advantage. Do not concentrate on misleading others but at least attempt to move to the control without attracting too much attention, punch your card and move away quickly. You will need to consult your map and compass immediately in order to proceed to the next control, but try to avoid being a focus of attention for the opposition. If necessary, move a little away from the control you have just discovered.

International Distress Signal

If you are a novice and apparently lost do not start blowing your whistle except as a last resort.

In the event of severe injury or getting completely lost towards darkness or the end of the Competition you would blow your whistle six times per minute and stay in one place for a long period to await help. Do not treat this lightly; try to find your bearings, or head in the direction of safety. You should have been given a safety bearing to travel if you get lost. It would be very unfair to expect serious competitors to come to your assistance just to find you had only been lost for a few minutes.

If you can find any control point stick rigorously to it if you are injured. The officials will soon be aware that you are missing because they are left with your Control card 'stub'. Stay on a track or wide path if possible because this will be the way the searchers will initially quarter the forest looking for you. Eventually all the Control sites will also be visited.

Juniors, please never offer help to find a Control, don't say 'it's down there', and please be very quiet at all Controls because in both instances you spoil the satisfaction of serious competitors who wish to find the Control markers themselves.

If there are several people arriving at a point together, you must be very quick to clip your own card and must avoid delaying others waiting to use the same clipper.

It is a pity that some unsociable people remove the clippers and sometimes even the markers from their position. If you are sure it has been removed then do not hang about, put a cross on your card in the empty box and carry on to the next control. Report the missing item immediately and when it is verified you will have your card initialled and accepted as if you had been able to clip it.

A relay change-over point

At the Finish

Everyone, it was pointed out, must report to the finish, but if you are sprinting to the finish funnel you must have your completed Control Card ready for handing over to the official. Sometimes in events your time is only noted down when your card is actually in the hands of the finish official. In a large event, although you will get a correct time for crossing the line, you must avoid spoiling the system. Be prepared to give your card to someone or for someone to give you a card with a time on it.

In each case always keep to the taped funnel and remain in line in the order of arrival among the other orienteers. Another helper will then ensure you have the proper time of finishing added to your Control Card as he collects it.

As the finish is a very busy place, move out of the way as soon as you have been dealt with and don't be surprised if your map is also temporarily removed from you. This is to avoid late starters from getting an advantage with a map preview.

When you have found your tracksuit or warm clothes, put them on immediately to avoid a chill and then go and help yourself to a drink. Orange juice is invariably free to all competitors but be careful of overdoing it. You will find the score board near at hand while you relax.

A scoreboard or results ladder

The Results Ladder

Each age section is listed and the names of each competitor per group are placed in order. The shortest winning time is at the top and with each new result the name and time is inserted at the correct position. It is easy for a late runner to do well and suddenly be placed at the top of the winning list and it is this that keeps up the tension to the last minute. Try to be available for the prize-giving even if you have not won a prize.

Techniques

All of the following ideas and hints are useful basic measures for improved times in your own personal performance. When you have been orienteering for a while you can apply to one of the regional organisations to attend one of their popular courses on improvement of technique. There are also courses on map making, course setting and competition organisation. There are plenty of more advanced books to master when you have finished this one. When you have been in several events try to take a good look at yourself, ask what are your weak points. You have to be able to read a map and all of the signs on it, you must be able to relate properly the map to the actual ground it shows and then you must be able to navigate to any place on that mapped area with the aid of distance measurement and direction measurement. Anyone can use a ruler in centimetres and millimetres and nearly everyone knows what a protractor is used for. If you give directions from Edinburgh to Glasgow you would say travel West for about 50 miles and you can't miss it. Naturally you gave a direction and a distance, so do not get all mixed up in orienteering when you have to be more precise.

Distance

The Bar Hill map (p. 114) has a scale of 1:10,000 which means 100 m on the ground is represented on the map by 1 cm.

In many situations you will need to calculate distances to see which is the best route choice and to see how many paces to count.
Here are three examples showing a choice; the direct route is shown as a solid line and the dotted route shows an alternative on p. 114. Which of the three direct route examples has been measured incorrectly? (X to X1 represents 160 m; Y to Y1 represents 510 m; Z to Z1 represents 180 m). If the orienteer decided it was better to skirt round that rough hilly part and follow the field boundary he would travel 330 m on the dotted 'X' route. Also on the 'Y' route he notices that he can follow the track and avoid the strip of forest but he must bear in mind that it will be 800 m on the dotted route.

Measure at Z and you find it is 300 m along the dotted route up the path. This must be worthwhile because the direct route passes through very dense forest described as 'fight' shown in dark green. I hope you measured the alternative dotted routes and spotted the deliberate mistake.

I hope these thoughts from the setter's ideas will help you to learn but better still if it stimulates you later to try to set a course for an event yourself.

Of course you will remember the maths teacher saying that the angle of a right-angle is 90° and the angle of a straight line is 180° and so on. It is therefore easy to imagine the four quarters as right-angled triangles and therefore N, E, S, W are like this.

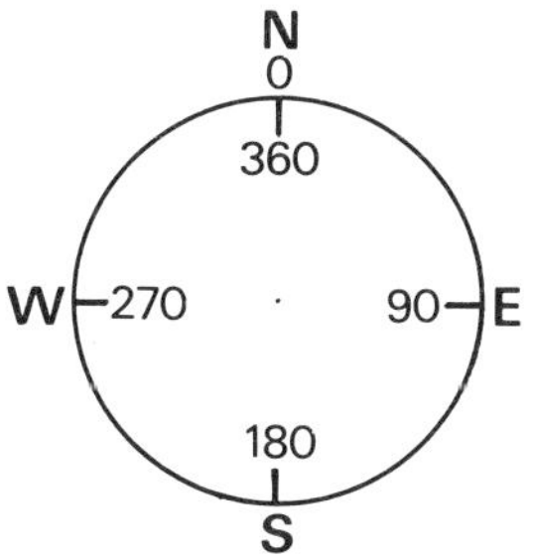

If you can't imagine it, then put two protractors together.
Now there's nothing new to do except adapt what you could do with your ruler and protractor.

◀ Think of two protractors

▼ A demonstration compass

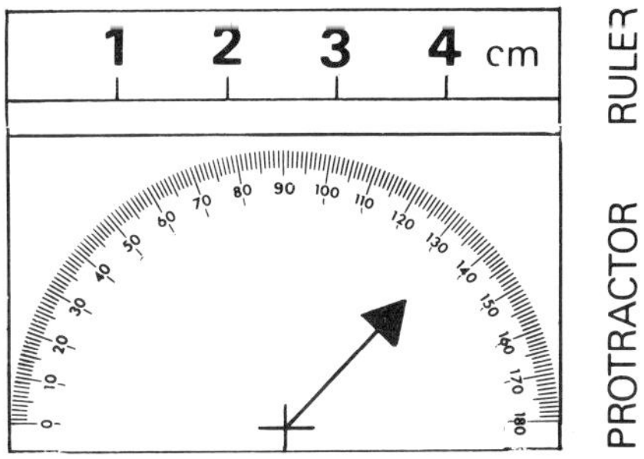

Direction Finding

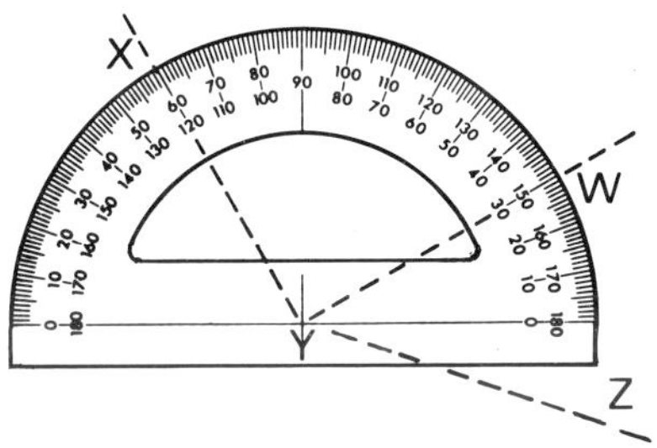

Using the line XX on the North Achray map (p. 115) you can see that the point R is 60° from the control point. Most people find school *protractors* easy to use, so using one would help you to measure accurately that the control at S is 140° from the base line. Since the line has been placed on top of the Magnetic North line you can see that T has an angle of 210° but this time you would use the protractor twice (180° + 30° = 210°). So if you look at the Silva Compass you should note how the dial has 360° marked on it for use in an easier manner. Read the instructions that come with your compass and the Silva method explains exactly how to find your direction.

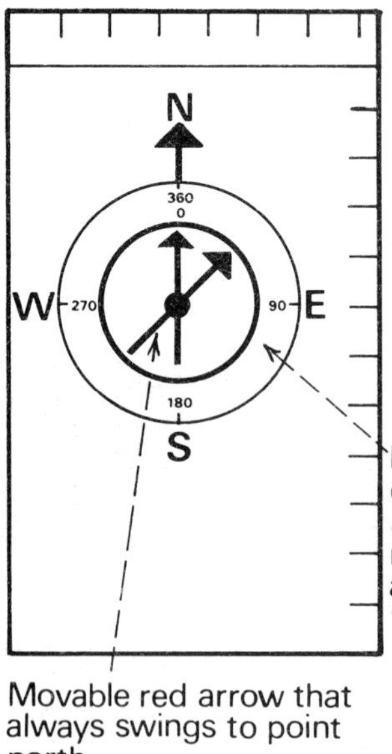

At first imagine your compass like this; then it is simple to go on to the whole thing

Aiming Off

The three controls marked A, B, C are all on line features on the North Achray map (p. 115) which are a stream, a ditch and a road. If a bearing was taken it would be worth 'aiming off' as indicated. Therefore the bridge at A is easily found by turning right when the stream is located. A direct aim would have left a doubt as to whether to turn left or right, if the bridge had not been spotted immediately on reaching the stream. Exactly the same problem is avoided by 'aiming off' to find B, the 'ditch junction', and to find Control C, at the correct passing place on the track. This is a very useful technique which can be used for finding attack points as well as the actual controls.

Getting the Map Pointing in the Right Direction

(see diagrams opposite)

You are coming down on a parachute and you see a large road to the front. Obviously if your map has only one road, it must be placed in the front as you point in the direction that you see the road (see photo on p. 52). In other words you get the map pointing in the correct direction. This is known as orientating the map. It would be quite wrong to have the map in any other direction.

Since you don't usually arrive at orienteering competitions by parachute you will not know what the aerial view looks like so you will have to fall back on using a compass.

All compass needles point to Magnetic North, which is slightly different from the direction of the North Pole.

Disorientated

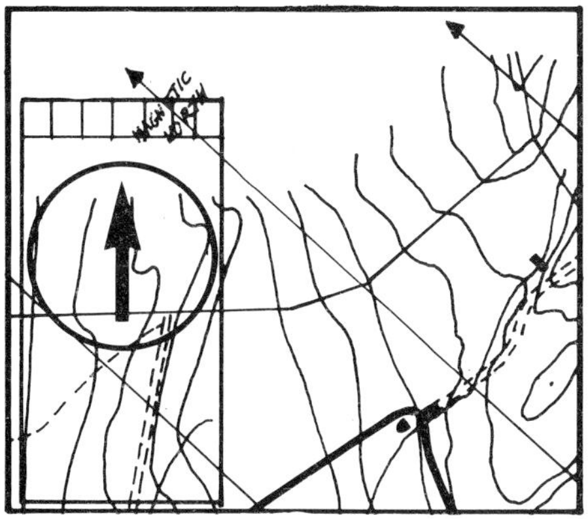

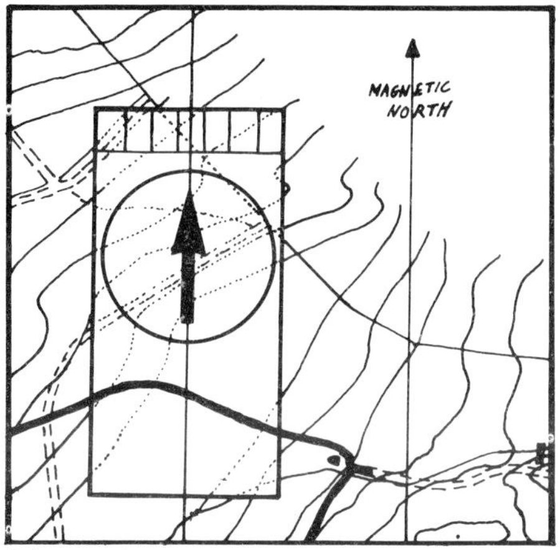

Orientated correctly

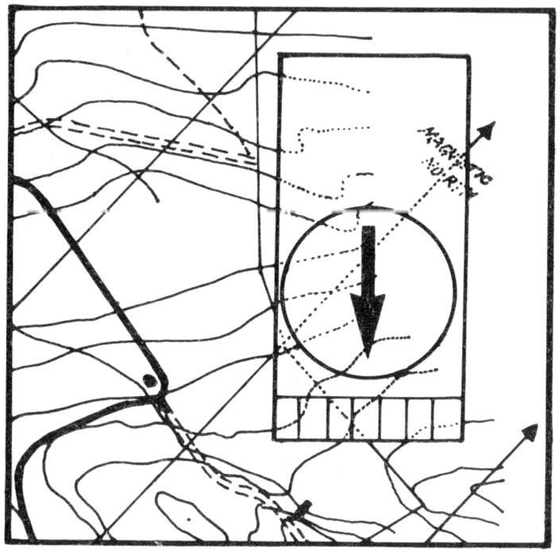

Disorientated

Using a compass is like using a protractor

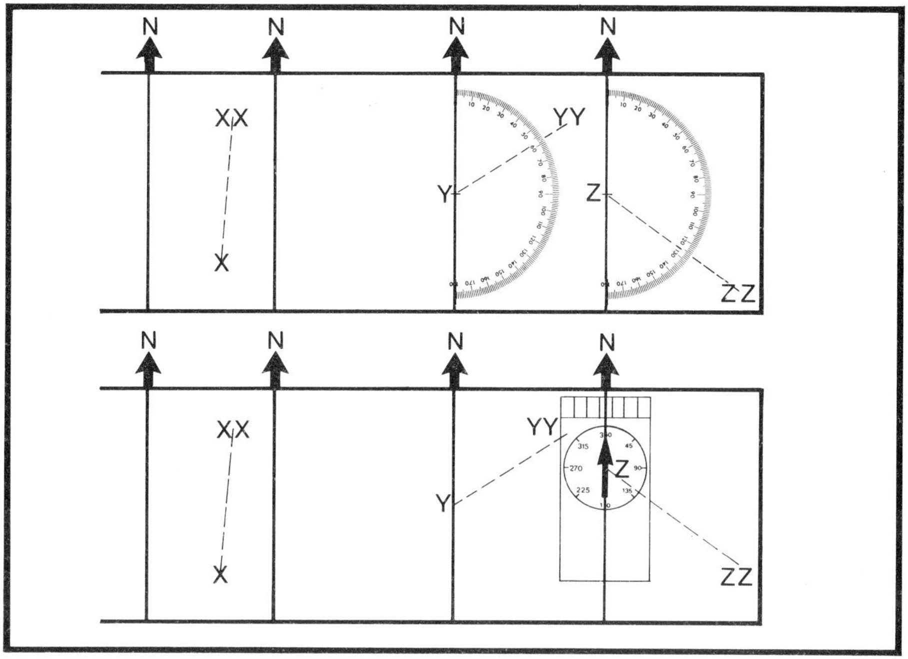

All 'O' maps have the Magnetic North direction lines drawn on them, so all you have to do is to get the compass's moving needle lined up with the Magnetic North lines on the map.
Thus all you have to do with a compass is to find out where the Magnetic North is situated so that the map is facing the correct way and then read off the angle. To avoid having to look through the needle and base plate, a movable dial is provided. Simply move the dial until the black diagram of an arrow is exactly under the moving red arrow which must still point along the Magnetic North lines accurately. The correct angle is displayed where it says 'Read bearing here'. My simple way to orientate the map or set the map with the ground is to get all **FOUR** arrows pointing the same way. This means moving the map until it is correct, with the three arrows on the compass in line with a North arrow on the map.

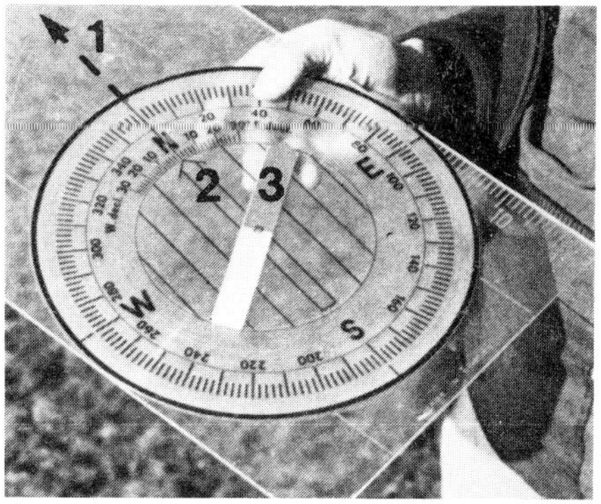

The three arrows

Arboricultural oddity or lone tree, written 'X' ▶

Always orientate your map whenever you are selecting which direction to travel. Course setters could bring you up to multiple tracks or ditch junctions and hope to tempt you up the wrong one.

Note that the needle will give a slightly wrong reading if the compass is not held level.

Do not forget that any metal object such as a fence or car may attract the compass needle and thus alter your proper line for Magnetic North.

However, when you are tired beware of having the needle back to front—IT IS ONLY THE **RED** END THAT YOU MUST USE FOR FINDING MAGNETIC NORTH.

Let us summarise. Whenever you look at the map, get the map facing the same way as the countryside it represents. To do this make the moving red arrow of your compass point exactly along the Magnetic North arrows shown running in parallel lines across your map. That means you can only rotate the map to get them to line up in a properly orientated way, so please don't forget to do it **every time** you stop to decide which way to go.

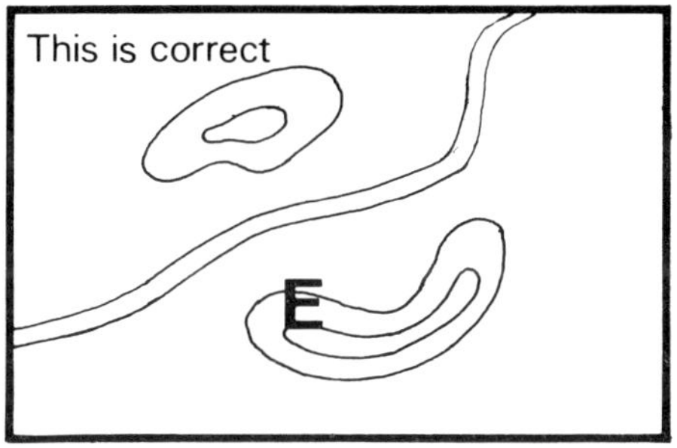

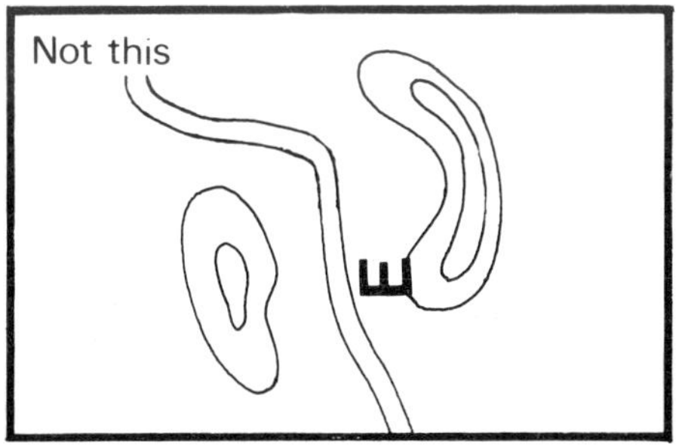

Remember to get the Magnetic North arrows on your map facing the North every time you look at it, this is called **orientating** the map. Look at the photo, now if you came down by parachute at E you would be able to orientate it by making sure the road was ahead of you.

When walking or running, start by looking in the exact direction with your compass held up to your eye and note the furthest recognisable point on that line. It may be a particular boulder or an odd shaped tree or a clump of bracken. Stop looking at the compass, run to your landmark; when you reach it look along the compass for the next landmark and run to it and so on. Bearings requiring travel more than about 200 m will not be accurate enough to pinpoint a feature. So now you can choose any route, measure its bearing and travel in the right direction on the actual terrain.

Pacing

You might be a giant or a dwarf so you **must** measure the length of your own paces at all speeds, such as sprint, fast stride, trot and walk. A man's running stride can be about 2 m but his walking stride might be only 1 m. He would therefore take about 100 strides running compared with 200 walking over 200 metres which is 1 cm on our map. So why not lay out marks at 200 m intervals in the forest that are flat, uphill or downhill and find out your own paces for 200 m. A very good tip is to paste this written information in the front of your compass so that when you measure distance on maps you actually read the number of steps rather than centimetres.

Add this information to your compass

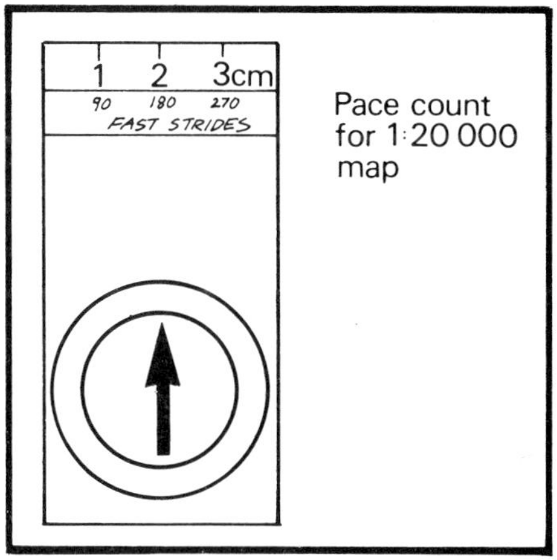

However, people of different age and sex vary in leg size and length of stride so you must go and work out your own particulars over differing terrain.

Even better data added

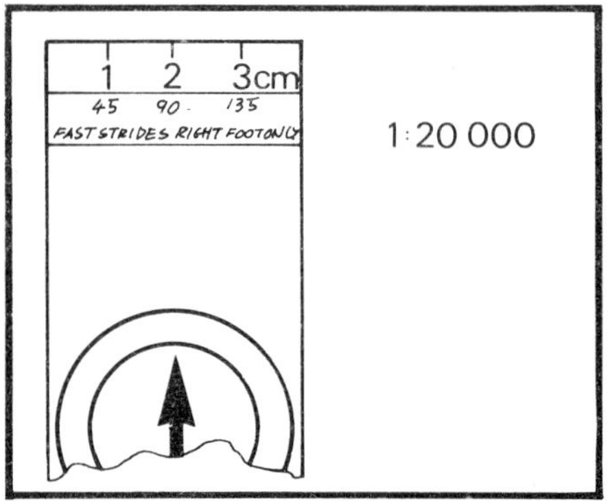

The author timed himself over 200 m as follows:

	Seconds	Paces	Increase
1. Flat	27	80	—
2. Hillside in woods	44	116	50%
3. Downhill	44	120	50%
4. Uphill	72	192	100%+

Your own information should become intuitive to you when making route choices, for example, it may well take you twice as long uphill as doing the same distance on the flat.

Counting every pace is a nuisance and orienteers tend to count every other one by counting each right foot step. So work out your own preferred method and stick to double paces if you wish. A tachometer or counter could be used to help you. So far we have only said assume 1 cm represents 200 m. This is one particular scale, otherwise written 1:20,000 which means 1 cm on the map represents 20,000 cm on the ground. Whoever heard of measuring a long distance in centimetres, it would be better to convert to metres by dividing by 100. Thus 1 cm on the map represents 200 m in the forest. This is the commonest scale used in orienteering and is rather close to the $2\frac{1}{2}$ in. to the mile used by the Ordnance Survey.

If someone gave you an orienteering map which was drawn at 1:10,000 you would just have to divide by 100 or take off the last two noughts. Thus 1 cm this time represents 100 m and this is a map twice the size and detail. So it means that your pace information must be halved if it has been pasted on to your compass.

This is a summary of what to do with your map.

1. Put red ink along your Magnetic North arrows if they are not easy to see.
2. Check scale. 1:20,000 means 1 cm represents 200 m; 1:10,000 represents 100 m and 1:22,500 225 m.
3. Orientate the map, i.e. face it towards the Magnetic North using the swinging compass arrow that always points at the Magnetic North.
4. Measure distance of your journey in centimetres and change it to metres or paces.
5. Nearly all orienteering can be done in the novice's events by just following line features e.g. walls, tracks, fences, edges of woods etc. A beginner only needs to be able to set or orientate his map at junctions. Occasionally he will use his compass to go from A to B as described in 6 below.

6. Place long base plate edge of compass in the direction you wish to travel. Turn the compass wheel until the lines on the base of wheel house are parallel with the Magnetic North lines on the map. Make sure that the arrow in the wheel house base points to Magnetic North on the map. Lift the compass off the map and turn with compass held steady in front of you, until the floating red arrow points in the same direction as the arrow on the bottom of the wheel house. Travel in the direction of the big arrow on the base plate where it says 'Read bearing here'.

   Anticipate what you will see next before you reach it and thus **keep in contact with the map** the whole time in order to ascertain your absolute location at all times. So remember **Orientate – Direction – Distance.** (O.D.D.)

So that is all the basic map technique except for learning all the signs, colours and codes and that is just homework which follows on p. 56.

Practical Course Guidance

Please check the course with your compass at North Achray (p. 115). It is meant only for practice and you could draw a course on a local map and try out your own technique in a small forest.

Always orientate the map to get it facing in the correct direction. To find Control 1, 'the clearing', just follow the track and turn right at the ditch. You still do not need your compass for following the ditch up to the crossing of the path and track. To go direct from this point to the small rock outcrop a bearing of 166° is needed. Keep to the right rather than the left if the trees force you off your line for then you can use the clearing to tell you if you have gone too far.

Leave Control 2 by running in line with the long crag until you reach the stream and path, try to follow the vegetation boundary to help you towards the forest road. Then take a 344° bearing to pass via the outcrop and use the large boulder as an 'attack point' to take a careful compass reading of 40° and thus walk the last 30 m to Control 3. Only map reading is needed to get close to Control 4, but 'attack' with a short bearing of 346° from the East end of the crags in order to find the clearing. Run fast to the road which is a

This forest area is 'walk', i.e. difficult obstacles

major feature you cannot miss, then run on a 40° bearing from the road at the passing place. It will help to 'aim off' deliberately to the South of Control 5 and first find the large stream. This will avoid any doubt whether you have reached one of the ditches instead of the stream. The final control can be approached from the track junction but a bearing must be taken, which is 12°, and then it is only 50 m to the depression. Now follow the tapes as fast as possible to the finish which you will see is exactly 70 m as shown by the 7 mm representation on the map.

Homework

Many other books describe training exercises which are of course very valuable such as miniature score events, point orienteering, and compass practice games like hunt the Silver Dollar. These are well documented in the excellent book **Orienteering** by John Disley. I shall not repeat the same material, excellent as it is, so you are well advised to read his book.

My contribution here is to teach you all the special map signs used for orienteering and to show you what they actually represent on the ground.

The numbers of the signs are those indicated on p. 113.

Yellow Homework

Look at the chart of symbols and make an effort to recognise them in the countryside. It would be helpful if you made your own photos and diagrams apart from the selection offered here.

One of the first surprises to new orienteers is that the forests are

Forest boundary—a thin yellow strip on the map, with yellow field areas beyond fence

always left colourless which is quite different of course from the ordnance survey where they are usually green areas. Since orienteering is very often in forests they are left colourless and clear of most named places to allow plenty of room for details of paths, tracks, streams and other features. Green is used for very dense areas of trees only.

Signs 18-20 The first sign here is for all open land. Now if you think about it, there will be quite a lot of clear areas in a large forest especially if it is being worked. The fields or moorland surrounding the forest will show as a broad band round the edge of the mapped area. It is quite likely that these are out of bounds, probably having a standing crop in them. Bear in mind too that the edge of the forest may well have a boundary fence. It can sometimes be profitable for orienteers to remember that a well kept forest area is usually brashed or cut back from the boundary. There is often, therefore, a very useful and easily travelled route along the inside of the enclosure.

Some parts of the woods may have been damaged by animals, floods, erosion or even by fire and so once again the mapper can use the yellow colour for clear areas. The fringe of the forest may be indistinct with a few trees dotted around the actual arable or pasture land at its perimeter. This sort of boundary area would make a fairly hard test of your navigating and step counting.

Quite often the actual forest limit is hard to decide on with strips of trees extending out from the main forest in several places. The boundary fence may now be in ruins in some places and sound in others. So make sure you learn these variations which may be quite difficult to distinguish.

Thinning ▼

Sign 21 You will find that forestry workers can fell trees faster than enthusiastic mappers can keep up-to-date. Hence the importance of reading and marking carefully any last minute map alterations which will be on view at the prestart or registration area. If you see evidence of work going on in the forest, then take it into account.

Most maps usually take at least a year to complete and they are expensive to print so don't be surprised to find changes at the last moment, shown on the master maps.

Thinning may well begin as in this picture but that may probably lead only to straight rides or thin pathways between the trees which are likely to be parallel with the

Ride junction ▼

▼ The wall and fence junction or overgrown ride

line of planting. This will not show as a yellow area or open ride unless the cutting is beyond about 15 m. Complete sections of forest may well have been removed and the map sign is easily recognised.

Sign 22 If you don't know what an orchard looks like you had better give up.

Sign 23 It is surprising how many forests overlook the sea or an estuary and appropriately enough a broad yellow band indicates the sand dunes or beach. Some dunes are enormous and are tremendous features for hanging control markers on. It is very difficult indeed to orienteer in sand dunes, especially during a night event, as they all look so similar. It is also very slow running, so if possible make your route avoid sand in favour of running in forest litter.

Sign 31 Be careful looking at the wide rides on your map. If you look carefully the yellow strip will have a series of very short dashes if the ride is extremely runnable. In your tired condition make sure it is not a series of long dashes (**Sign 32**) because this could indicate an overgrown old ride looking just like the above picture. Naturally this is where the fit alert orienteer will gain vital minutes. In some cases it might be worthwhile using the overgrown ride, at least you can follow it and may not need your compass until you reach the next feature.

Sign 40 This can be evident when there are roads dividing large forests; small hamlets are always close to the main road and would be avoided when the organisers were planning the event. Nevertheless, remember that cross hatching of various sizes indicates inhabited areas, and the name of the hamlet will probably not even be printed. In an emergency this information might well be vital so don't neglect to learn it too.

Sign 41 This is self-explanatory and indeed very rare in an orienteering map. (Dare I suggest it might be an indication of the dead centre of the map!)

Some commonly met features with which you must be familiar

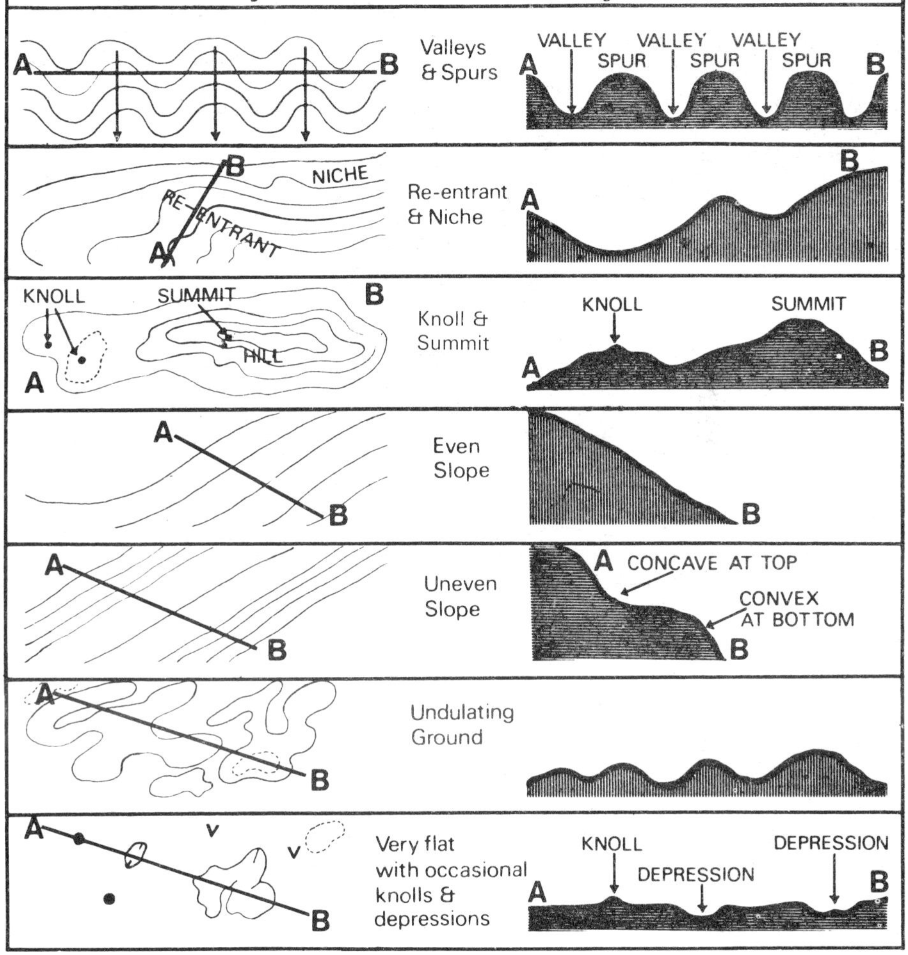

Not a comprehensive coverage of all the various countour features likely to be encountered, but sufficient for the beginner

As early as possible you must recognise examples 'in the field' and develop the skill of visualising these features in your mind when you see their contour patterns

Brown Homework

Contours show the relative heights of the land; each line usually represents 5 m of height, so 10 lines close to each other will be 50 m high. If these 10 lines were spread out on the map they would still represent only 50 m in height, but of course, they would not be so steep.

Sign 1. This shows three regularly spaced Brown lines showing an even slope. To the left are two circular lines, these are both showing the same height, which would mean that the hill has two small summits of equal height.

Sign 2. This is an even slope. Note the major contour, every fifth one is darker but is 25 m higher. Note the slight bend in each contour, this shows a slightly lower area or groove in the hillside.

One kink in one contour is sometimes called a niche and is quite hard to find in the ground, it is like a dent a few metres across. Large valleys show a whole series of kinks on each successive contour. The orienteer has to decide if contours are too close together for his comfort. He must consider whether the hill will be too steep and slow compared with making a longer detour.

'Large Knoll (North side)' or perhaps 'The Spur'

'The Knoll' or 'Crag Foot', or 'Boulder Field'

'The Bank (South side)' or 'The Depression (2 metres deep)'

Sign 3. The form line is shown as an occasional set of brown dashes between contours. This shows awkward lumps and bumps on hillsides that are say 22 m high or 54 m, i.e. they would appear on the 20 or 50 m contour but not on the 25 or 55 m contour. Thus a general impression of the lie of the land is indicated by a form line. It could not be described as a control point as such.

Sign 4. The Knoll, shown as a Brown dot, small ring contour or form line. There are seven in this diagram. They are all shapes and sizes, some have trees, some do not; they are on hillsides, in fields and hidden in the forest. Really large ones require the Setter to indicate the position of the marker, e.g. The Knoll, East side. They make useful attack points.

Sign 5. The Depression is a hole in the ground like a bomb crater, large or small. The large type may be 20 m across and you might have a job getting out, but a really difficult depression to find might only be about 4 m wide and covered with undergrowth. Very accurate bearings are usually needed to locate them. The map sign is V-shaped or sometimes like an egg cup.

Sign 6. A gully is a sharp gash in the hillside and may not be very large hence this special sign. You should think twice about using them for a route, it might be hard work.

Sign 7. In forests there are often long earth banks, ancient earth forts, anti-tank ditches and all sorts of peculiar man-made embankments. The sign looks like a Brown comb or fence but remember the lengths are accurate according to the map scale.

Sign 8. A Black fence-like sign means a crag, small ones of only 3 m high often occur in the woods. It is really a small cliff, possibly partly moss covered and no problem to negotiate. Avoid long crags shown along sets of very close contours because these are likely to be impassable cliffs and your route must go elsewhere. The quarry shown is usually a half circle of fence signs, the site may be active and 30 m deep or it might be an ancient quarry all overgrown and barely 8 m high.

Sign 9. The boulder field will make dreadful running as it will more than likely contain rough gravel or moss covered slippery rocks on the ground between the giant boulders.

◀ Sign 6. 'The Gully' or 'On the Stream Bend', or 'The Boulder' or perhaps 'The Waterfall'

Sign 7. 'Steep Slope'

Sign 8. 'The Cliff Foot'

Sign 8. 'The Crag Foot (East side)'

Sign 9. 'The Boulder Field'

◀ This is actually 'The Wall'—a broken part admittedly; or 'The Marsh' or 'The Spring'. (Signs 35 or 15 or 13.) All these features occur together here

Blue Homework

Sign 10. The spring is a place where water bubbles or seeps out of the ground or rock. Note the difference between the sign for the stream which is permanent water and the ditch which is shown as Blue dots. These make very useful routes through dense forest and save tremendous amounts of time. They are often dry except after rain. Try not to damage the banks. Judge the type of ground when following streams because very steep untended forest may well be neglected and what looked like a good short cut might turn out to be a nightmare of washed down rubble and logs.

Sign 11. This sort of feature is probably a river that is 5 or 10 m wide and you must quickly look for bridges on the map, so that your route includes them.

These runners were looking for 'On the Bridge' but their map-reading should not have led them to this path under the bridge

Sign 12. Look closely to see the bridge on the stream and the dotted Black line showing the path along the stream past the waterfall and over the bridge. That lake or loch might be a nuisance if you find yourself on the wrong side due to bad route choice. It might be jungle right down to the waterline, followed by a wall of 2 m bullrushes so read your map first.

Sign 13. See the Blue egg cup shape for the source or starting point of a stream. This might be completely overgrown or it might be only evident in the winter, so do not be misled if the area is dry or if the stream goes underground again close by.

A well can be many things: A brick built construction; a hole with corrugated iron over it, a concreted cover or just a very small puddle of water. So rely on your map reading to find it rather

'The Loch (East Bank)' (Sign 12) ▶

than have a preconceived idea of what the well should look like. The tank is probably a big iron framed box about 3 m long and 2 m wide. The idea is often to collect rain water as a source for fire fighting. Sometimes it may be a concrete settling tank for somebody's domestic water supply.

Sign 14. Uncrossable marsh means what it says, a swamp, and the Setter does not want you near it. Note the solid black line round the edge indicating its nasty nature.

Sign 15. A friendly marsh if you like that sort of thing. It shows no boundary as you can see, but you will certainly be wet up to the ankles if you think the short cut worthwhile.

Sign 16. The same thing in Brown means a wooded area with soggy ground under it. It might help to check your bearings so look out for marsh plants such as reeds and sedges or perhaps an odd willow tree.

Sign 17. The next sign says seasonally dry, which means it may be dry in summer.

'The Depression' or 'The Pit' (Sign 5) ▶

'On the Bend (Forest Road)' (Sign 26)

Black Homework

Sign 24. The figures 1:20,000 are the scale, and **must** be on the map. Remember—take off two noughts and you have the number of metres represented by each centimetre measured on the map, i.e. 200.

Sometimes 1:25,000 and quite often the much more detailed 1:15,000 or 1:10,000 map is used in orienteering.

Sign 25. A metalled road has a double Black line to represent it. It is a proper road for cars, and is made of tarmac.

Sign 26. A thick Black line is a forest road or unmetalled farm road which is suitable for vehicles but is generally unmade and bumpy. They are built to remove timber with lorries and tractors and provide easy running for orienteers.

Sign 27. Not suitable really for anything but tractors but note that all the following signs show dots or dashes of different sizes. These sizes are agreed conventions and the size of mapping pens are always specified in the B.O.F. mapping booklets, so try to recognise them.

▲ 'Path Junction' or 'Bank End' (Signs 28 or 38)

'The Path Bend' (Sign 29)

'The Stream'. This is what is known as 'Fight', as shown in dark green. Avoid it

Sign 28. The sort of path you might ride a horse down or with difficulty push a pram.

Sign 29. Very small black dots denote a twisty, uneven path among the trees. It has probably been made by animals or forestry workers and will make an excellent route for a mobile orienteer. Probably no use at all even for a horse as it might be overgrown or pass under low trees and bushes.

Sign 30. A ride is what it says, a place for horses only. Wheeled vehicles would be impeded by boulders or fallen tree trunks, marshy areas and other difficulties.

Sign 31. The wide ride could be about 5 or 10 m wide and as you can see if it is not rough it shows short dashes. Note the yellow strip, to denote that vegetation has been cut right back; probably its original function was that of a firebreak between separate sections of the forest.

Sign 32. The long dash on the Yellow line indicates the same as sign 31, but it has been neglected and overgrown. Perfectly feasible for orienteers but you will expect to dodge round a few gorse bushes, under fallen trees and wade deep in old bracken.

Sign 33. The power line is an excellent collecting feature and also it is very often kept clear of all vegetation except moss and ferns and therefore makes better travelling than through dense young fir trees. Each Z on the map usually marks the exact position of the pylons so they also act as a useful string of attack points.

Sign 34. Don't hang about here, you might be accused of hitching a lift.

Sign 35. The boundary is a solid line unless it is in ruins. You might well come unstuck in an event if you assume you can cross it because it might be a deer fence. Sometimes it is wire strands, wire netting, moss covered fallen stones, wooden fencing and is often difficult to locate in some old sections.

Sign 36. This sign either means physically impossible to cross or it might be meant as out of bounds. Do you see the tiny gap of the crossing points, which is a gate or sometimes it is a frightening ladder over the top of a deer fence.

Sign 37. Big old pine trees are easy to recognise, and if they were next to, for example, a young plantation of spruce the points that they meet at would be mapped with these tiny dots. A vegetation boundary will only be mapped if the tree types are very obviously different. It is a boundary and would also refer to a change from trees to a gorse area or to indicate clearings of large extent. Many maps do not include this sign, but if they do, make sure it is printed in black.

Sign 38. These small Brown dots show earth banks and long mounds which are less than a metre high. Again, they are excellent control points usually because they are found deep inside the forests and demand exacting compass work to locate them if they are short. Long ones naturally act as collecting features or are useful for running parallel to them to locate other points.

Sign 39. The North meridian is a Black or Blue line and can often be confused for a track, or stream, especially when the orienteer is tired. If they are not clear then ink them over, preferably in Red, so that you can place your compass straight onto them when orientating your map.

▲ 'The Tower' or 'The Ruins'. This area should be avoided or patrolled, or marked with yellow tapes (Sign 42)

'The Trig Point' (Sign 43) ▼

Sign 40 and 41. Yellow.

Sign 42. Ruins are sometimes so bad that only a quarter of one house wall remains. It will be covered in ivy or moss, there may be a tree fallen over it and it generally looks nothing like an old building so, again trust your map, not your eyes.

Sign 43. Trig points are places

Another 'X'—a pheasant cage (Sign 47) ▶

that O.S. mappers and surveyors have very accurately marked. They were used to set the position of all the other places on the map; very often a concrete pillar or a metal plate is erected on the site, which is usually a hill top. The **exact** height is frequently written on the map, e.g. 1016 ft. on an O.S. map. The contour dimensions can be calculated from these points if there is insufficient labelling on the map. Single boundary stones are very hard to find, so extra markers may be placed nearby.

Sign 44. These signs refer to peculiar features such as tall animal feeding baskets for feeding, presumably, tall animals! Towers are for fire watching; there are large water holding towers, tourist observation platforms and frequently high seats for hunters to look down and shoot safely towards the ground. All are shown by the letter T.

Sign 45. Keep away! The Controller would probably recommend Yellow Danger Signs or even an official to guard it.

Sign 46. I suggest you do not pick up anything you find, if the Army are running an event on their home territory. The dimensions of the shooting banks or butts will be accurately mapped, so it is quite feasible to take bearings from their ends.

Sign 47. The X is any other odd feature. It could be a rubbish dump, a memorial seat, even an old gravestone, often a dumped vehicle and occasionally the much revered arboricultural oddity. This means a single tree species that is obvious, such as a large Beech tree among the Conifers or an isolated dead tree trunk in a healthy young plantation.

Please do not forget to learn all the map signs and colour codes shown so well at the bottom of the Brownmuir map (p. 116) and on p. 113.

Novices' Walk

Using p. 117 to illustrate the principles let us assume a group of novices walking round together. (In practice, this actual course should not be attempted in one session because of the time that would be taken.) They will also need to refer constantly to p. 113 to learn the symbols.

Black

Drive to the loch and leave the minibus until we return near the road junction. Run to the wall and wait at the first track leading away from the wall towards the North.

Black
Black on Yellow
Blue

Now follow the wall for 200 m until we reach the ride. Then walk to the forest track up the hill and see who can find the source of the stream.

Let us now maintain height and go around the hillside to find the head of the ditch. That

Brown
Blue
Blue

sign is a formline which indicates the slight gully sloping down to the ditch. It is called a formline because it shows a form or shape which is not high enough to appear in the next higher contour. This must be why the drain was built, to collect extra rain here. Let's follow the ditch to the next stream and downhill again to the long wall. Look at that boulder field up there. We can call this wall a collecting feature since it collects us again and prevents us from losing our way. We would not miss it if we went South, S.W. or S.E.

Right follow the wall, run on and see who can find the next stream, wait at it, but in any case do not leave this straight wall.

Black

Next we will go up the vegetation change where Spruce changes to Pine to the North-East, until we reach the large clearing and find out what is at X. It could be

X Black

•• Black

anything but it happens this time to be a fire ladder; well on now past the two boulders and across the shallow valley to the wall corner. Let's follow the compass on bearing 78° to see how close we can come out of the trees to see the wall corner.

 Brown

Now just look at that beautiful view down the hill. It will be a fairly long walk again 'contouring' to reach the summit of the largest hill along this chain; we will not need to lose any height and will only have to climb about 8 m to reach the knoll on the top. Be careful to avoid that crag.

 Brown

 Brown

 Black line round yellow area

Looking North along the top or spur of the hill we can see to the left a small valley beginning, let us head down it to those fields.

 Blue

We've made a mistake because of the marsh, it's crossable but we will get wet feet so let's follow the edge of the woods, i.e. the vegetation boundary then cross the ride to find that depression.

 Black

V Brown

Now it should be simple to follow the stream.

Oh well, another mistake; it's too rough. This shows that streams are often not the best route to take.

O Blue

Feeling thirsty, then you can have a race across the field to the well. Now that's a bit different from the sort Jack and Jill were visiting. Remember this when you are in a competition because controls do not always look as you would expect.

T Black

Now continue on to T, which is a Tower or High Seat for shooting deer.

Did anyone see what was at X?

 Brown

Yes, it was a derelict car among the trees near that long earth bank. If you climb up that High Seat you can just catch a glimpse of the large waterfall over to the West.

 Blue

That's the one you can hear.

 Brown

Follow me over the embankment; that would make a good orienteering control point; let us walk through the trees, even

 Brown

though it is marshy, the map says it is crossable.

It is about halfway and time to go home so run on now along this stream until you come to the strange walled-in wood. I'll see you at the arch where the path comes out of the overgrown enclosure; it was probably a country house originally and that is the old walled garden.

 Black and Yellow

If we now cross the field, it will start getting steep so we will head for that wide ride.

 Black

We'll stop long enough to find that giant boulder.

Looks as if we are getting collected again by that helpful wall, so follow it until the third ride on the left. This will be in 550 m time, then follow bearing

 Black

300° and I'll see you at the trig point at the top of the hill.

If you climb a tower here you can see miles of rolling forest and it will convince you how important map reading and the compass are.

By the way, what is the bearing from the Trig Point to that Tower? The next bit is tricky so we will follow that little path, it would be helpful too in a competition.

 Black

It is actually a vegetation change as shown on the map.

Up the road, that tells us that we are exactly correct on the map because our path is coming in on the bend just as it does on the map. The rest is easy, follow the rides to the cart track, watch out for a big knoll in the clearing on the way and then find the crag foot.

● Brown

Black

Now it is all downhill to the loch for a rest and our sandwiches.

Next time, we will send you off in pairs and see what happens to you!

(See p. 118). **Stage 2.**

Let us now deal with more experienced novices and assume they are now getting to grips with maps and the 'O' symbols. Take them back to the area where the walk took place and set them off in pairs, on a course specially designed to give them confidence.

Laura and Linda are given the course and stay together except when they disagree about the route; they must wait for each other at each control to save getting lost.

From the start at the edge of the field Laura follows the edge of the forest to the North, crosses the road and climbs up the ride and takes the junction to the right. The angular bend is easy to find and she remembers to check her paces, so Control 1 is easily found.

▲
Laura

Linda

Linda was more courageous and headed straight to Control 1 by way of the steep path and took the bearing of the path. She then followed the same line using her compass through the open wood as she knew she had the ride as collecting feature as they were previously taught. Little surprise to her that she was there first and able to hide close to the control, much to Laura's disappointment later when she popped out. Linda was then able to help Laura with her compass when they both agreed on the direct route to the Summit. They remembered to **aim off** to the right by a few degrees so that they would hit the ride just below and to the right of the narrow path up to the summit and Control 2.

Next, the Crag. And they both decide to race each other to it. It is only at the ride crossing that they choose different routes.

Laura approached from the North and got all mixed up on the wooded slope near the Crag.

Linda, however, showing her skill again, followed the ride to the South and took the third path up the hill. After about 200 m she was able to look down on the control, which she remembered she had been told was preferable to being beneath a control.

There was another Crag at Control 4 and this time Laura was really determined to regain her pride, so she took a straight route with a compass bearing keeping one eye on the old wall to her left and maintaining height. However, she missed the Crag and had to stop at the junction of the two walls which pleased her to think that she had been **collected** even though she had missed the Control. She knew exactly where she was and was able to take the

back bearing by adding 180° to her previous direction. This time, she took 40 right foot large paces as she had been shown because it was 4 mm on the map which represented 80 m on the ground. She knew her steps were less than a metre and wished she had previously practised to find out the number of her own paces in 100 m (i.e. half a centimetre on the 1:20,000 map). Anyway, a **square Search** soon located the Control and she was indeed first there.

Meantime, Linda had chosen a route that measured about the same distance of approximately 650 m to the Crag but had neglected to study the contours.

She soon realised her mistake as she struggled to the top of the hill and then followed the path down to the bottom again. She was tired and walked the last bit from her chosen **attack point**. She had taken a bearing of 5° from the ride to the South of Control 4.

The girls had learnt a lot by now and decided to have a walk down to Control 5 and exchange ideas on how to reach No. 6. When they crossed the field they found the

Control called the track bend at the bottom of the sloping field.

The rivalry had now really set in so again they challenged each other to be first at No. 6. Laura went back up the forest track, passed through the trees near the waterfall and cut South for 30 m on the tiny path. She was really getting the hang of things now and intercepted the bank which she knew led towards No. 6, the old car.

Linda arrived almost simultaneously as she had cut across the marsh, jumped two streams and had used the deer shooting ladder (T) to keep her direction which she knew anyway (204°). Besides, it was exactly 120 metres past the ladder to the X on the map.

With the next leg all they had to do was follow the road for 600 m (3 cm). So they decided to work out their own number of paces. Linda **ran** and counted 340 steps which was 170 right foots. Laura **walked** and did 620 steps with 310 right foots. So they were able to work out that each centimetre on a 1:20,000 map was about 60 right foots when Linda **ran** and about 100 right foots when Laura **walked**. They easily found the pond by walking along the stream which cut the road by the ride.

The final control now became a real challenge and they had to meet each other at the waterfall. Linda, fresh from a rough climb, took the route round the hill and avoided a lot of climbing by **contouring**. Laura chose the route up the ride to the trig point, it looked easy on the map but it was so steep she wished she had taken notice of Linda's earlier experience. She certainly needed a rest when she arrived second at the falls.

At last the home run in, but they agreed to walk together to the top of the large spur. From there it was —may the best girl win and they rushed downhill to the finish at the car park marked on the map. They both came in from different directions simultaneously and agreed on a draw, with a definite challenge to beat each other in the local club contest they knew was being run the following week on the same map and area. They both agreed they had learnt a lot and were determined to join an orienteering club, so that they could learn more on a personal performance course. In the meantime, they would both be competing against each other in all the future contests. No more running in pairs for them, there just had to be a winner.

Navigating Hints

Aiming Off

Now that you have learnt to take a bearing and can follow it to find a control point you will have to realise that a straight line can sometimes be confusing. If you have to find a control point on a long line feature such as a stream or a path which you are approaching from one side then it will be impossible to know your exact position. (Diagram 1.)

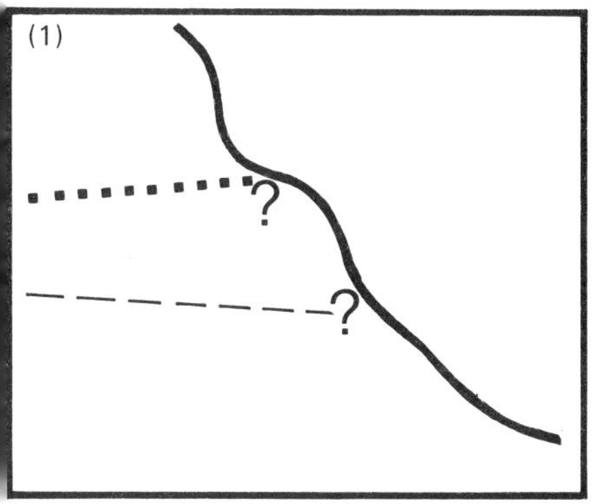

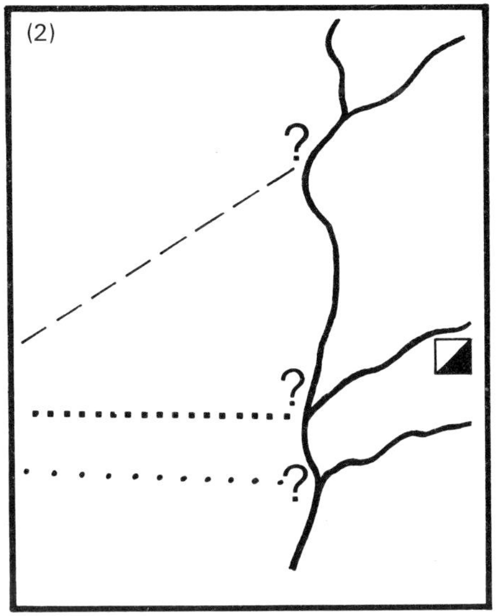

Searching for a stream junction you have a problem like this if you aim directly at it. (Diagram 2.)

It is very difficult to travel straight in forests hence you will be in Diagram 3 slightly out of line and therefore present yourself the problem of knowing which way to turn, as you will not be sure whether you are at A or B. You cannot afford that sort of time loss and should avoid the doubt by **deliberately** aiming at say A. This distance MUST leave you in no doubt that you are too far **UP** the stream when you get there. You will know that you turn right as soon as you see the stream. For the last part cut across the corner and again aim off slightly, instead of following the stream. (Diagram 4.)

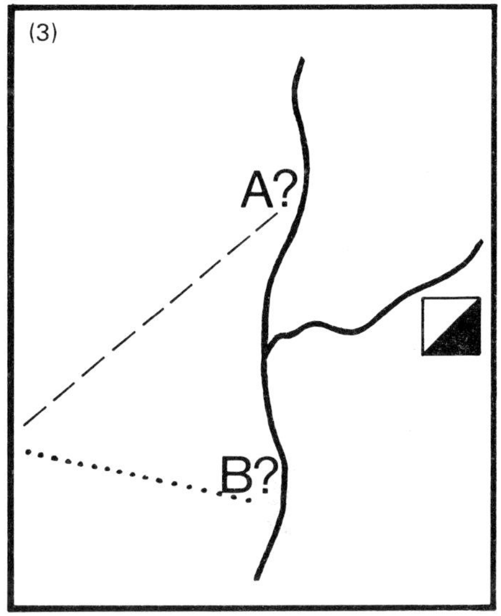

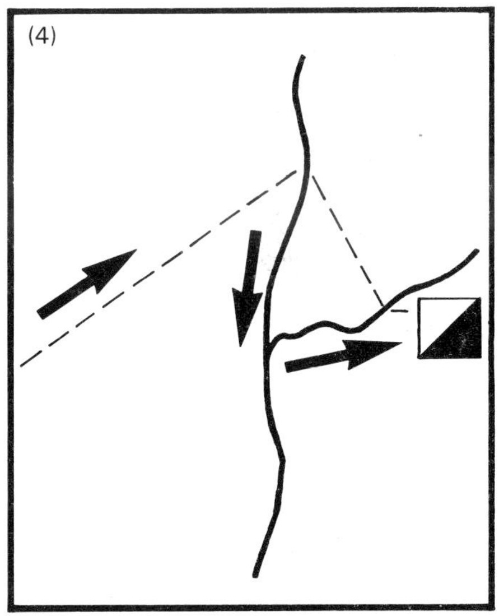

Of course you may need to adopt this technique when looking for points **other** than control points in order to find your way so it is quite often possible to use it.

Attack Point Theory

It is easy enough taking a bearing on a fixed feature but sometimes a Control is in the middle of the forest with no obvious stream or path going right up to it.

Lost

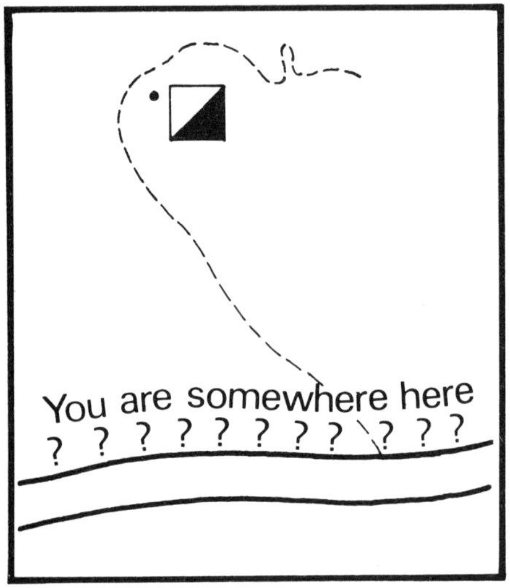

No exact bearing is possible and if you try to find this knoll you could so easily just miss it. Then you think you will have a little wander as it must be close and hey presto you are pretty well lost.

All you could do is return to the track and start again—so don't fall into that trap. I expect you will have to learn the hard way before you believe me though!

Do it the right way, look carefully at your map for the nearest absolutely definite point that you can be sure of finding.

Accurate

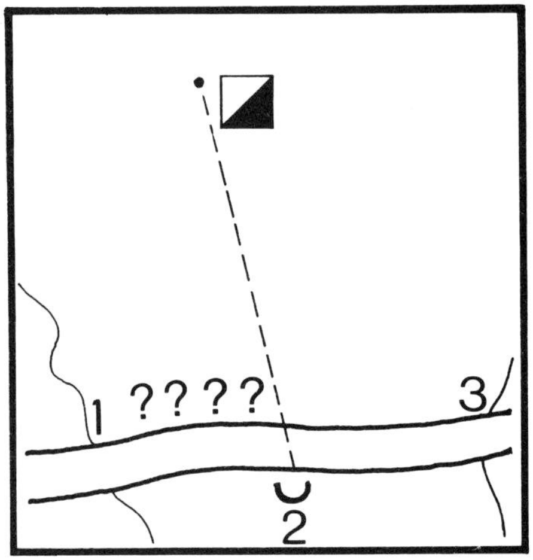

In this case there are three attack points 1, 2 and 3. A bearing must be accurately taken on your map and then you will walk on the exact bearing, having calculated the exact number of paces. No. 2 is the best attack point because the depression is easy to find as it is so close to the track. The bearing and distance will then bring you very close indeed to the Control point that you are searching for.

Attack Points on the Map

This really means absolutely identifiable spots that can be easily found and are therefore imperative for using as exact reference points. In this way you know without doubt where your bearing starts and finishes and the distance will tell you where you are on that line on the map. It cuts out doubt and guesswork.

Our friend the setter may hope you will be able to spot useful attack points so let us illustrate them. An attack point is a **fixed** point on a map that helps you find accurately another place. Control E, 'the marsh', on p. 114, can be reached in many ways but what a terrific 'attack point' is illustrated by that path shown arrowed. When you get to the path end you cannot fail to find the control.

Now here is a more difficult 'attack point' to grasp. If you look at the point of the arrow on the way to F, the green wood is very thick but the white wood is very open and easy to run through. This is a 'vegetation boundary' and is helpful because when you

reach it you could follow it down to the fence shown and would then be 20 m from the pond. Even the junction of fence and vegetation boundary gives you a very good 'attack point' for a bearing of 100° to the pond. (The other arrow shows another possible attack point to follow the stream.)
Similarly, either end of the marsh would be useful to take a bearing from to reach the crag at G. Although this feature is so large it hardly needs a bearing, simply go 60 m from the path at right-angles as soon as you reach the N.E. end of the marsh.

Contouring

This means following the slope of a hillside that will act as a guide to the next control or attack point. The Brownmuir Map (p. 116) shows the idea from A to B although on this map it shows open country and in this case it would be easy to look down to find the boulder by using the direct route. You can see the contours easily in this demonstration and a runner would follow round the curve of the hillside until he found the crag, then by climbing about 15 m after finding the crag he could contour again to reach the two boulders.

Route Choice

The Setter tries to arrange that each leg presents several routes to choose from; there is thus a possibility that a runner may make a bad choice and lose time finding out his mistake.

A good hint is to work **backwards**, look **first** at the Control you wish to reach, then working back find the available attack points. When this decision has been made it is usually fairly easy working out how to reach the attack point. Work back to the previous Control and in fact look before you leap, but good orienteers try to stick to the idea that the shortest distance between two points is a straight line, so avoid excessive detours unless you have a good reason.

Much practice can be done at home, such as reading a map and working out potential route choices. If you set courses, it is very good experience for learning how the Setter must think so that when you are competing you may anticipate the problems that he will arrange.

The orienteer has to choose his route carefully comparing distances, comparing the height to be climbed and the difficulty of travel. Practise your own travel rate and write down your personal speeds for passing along flat paths versus travelling through open forest. Compare the latter two easy terrains with uphill forest travel, with passage through very dense undergrowth and with downhill wooded conditions. The combinations are innumerable but at least try to remember your own rate for flat versus uphill and for open versus dense vegetation.

Small Hints to Save Seconds

1. An oil-filled compass is better than an ordinary one because the oil makes the needle stop swinging rapidly.
2. Use 'transpaseal' or transparent waterproof material to protect your control card and map from the damp.
3. Important. Ignore everyone else and all verbal advice—which could well be misleading.
4. Practise map memory—remembering the terrain ahead after reading your map.
5. Add a pace guide to your compass to avoid calculations.

Practice

You will be surprised to see how long it takes to do the following two exercises which you are advised to try:

1. Time yourself while measuring the distance and the bearing of all 12 controls as a home test on the map of Brownmuir (p. 116).
2. Put a control mark and a clipper punch at the bottom of your garden, then repeat exercise 1 but run and clip your card between each measurement. Improvement in this will of course pay dividends in time saving in an actual event. Try it please.

Waiting for their start time

Organisation of Large Badge Event

As soon as the orienteer feels competent, he should offer to help organise events, because they take up so much time if only a few people help to run them. If organisers are overworked they may eventually give up doing it but if the work is shared it becomes a pleasure to organise or set an event. Apart from that, a novice will learn a tremendous amount in this way.

At least a year ahead of a proposed event the area chosen must be visited to examine the forest as it will look next season.

Obviously the condition of the undergrowth, the height of bracken, the amount of water in the ditches, etc., are all important to know about. Therefore the first consideration really is the feasibility of the forest area to be used.

When the area is agreed as suitable the most urgent task is to obtain permission from the landowner or from the Forestry Commission if they own it. Of prime importance is the parking potential and the avoidance of traffic problems and the creation of hazards to vehicles and competitors.

So a reconnaissance is carried out and it is found from the map that there are only, for example, three easy access tracks for competitors to enter the woods. These are probably forest tracks with gates. The competitors will not be allowed to drive cars inside the forest but it will be desirable for a few officials to drive in with equipment, the complete set of control markers, refreshments and first aid. Similarly an emergency vehicle could remove an injured person more easily if access is available directly to the forest.

Since forest roads are built for removal of products and for fire prevention, access is usually at least partly available.

Parking. Often the greatest trouble is to obtain adequate parking facilities. So look for a realistic parking area, capable of taking an adequate number of cars and don't forget all the coaches, although these can drop passengers and wait elsewhere if necessary. It is well worth hiring a field for your peace of mind but it must have a very good access and of course not be wet. Thank the farmer, preferably in writing, a token fee being normal.

Forester. Consult the local forester about the possibility of using the forest and see if there are some areas that should be out of bounds or that competitors should be directed away from, e.g. young trees. This can be done by intelligent course setting. Ask him for the correct name of his forest section and ask your regional Fixtures Secretary to apply to the regional Forestry H.Q. for a permit to use the area.

The Commission. You will almost certainly get permission from the conservator in the form of a standard typed permit. This confirms the date, place and conditions of the competition.

Usually it refers to a shooting tenant who also has to be consulted for permission to use the forest, thus ensuring that he will not be out shooting orienteers on that day!

The Permit. This will ask for insurance cover for damage to the forest by fire. The insurance is automatic as soon as an event is registered together with details. 'The Orienteer' and regional newsletters will publicise the event which is an essential part of the agreement with the insurers. The insurance also covers damage done by officials prior to the event, whilst surveying, mapping, and controlling.

Besides the Commission, the estate owner also is usually worried about insurance, damage and litter, so again the organiser must take care of these matters before and after the day.

Delegation. The organiser will soon be a nervous wreck unless he soundly delegates **all** of the jobs involved. This will leave him free on the day for checking all positions and covering any last minute problems!

He is likely at first to appoint the best **'setter'** available, and if the latter agrees the competition planning, the actual marking of the course and the final removal of controls can be left to him. This is obviously a tremendous weight off the organiser's mind.

Controller. The organiser will now seek a very experienced orienteer and ask him to control or 'oversee' the whole event. The Controller will already be well known for putting on large successful races and will have passed the official B.O.F. exam and will be on the official list of Graded Controllers. It will be reasonable to try to match the Controller and Setter in temperament to ensure that they can co-operate together over the months. This man has the absolute final word on **every** stage and aspect of the event, and may have travelled a long way, so make sure he is kept informed of all matters as they happen and also ensure his expenses are repaid.

Mapping Team. These volunteers will need to survey the total area and should be in liaison with the

Setter. If some areas are very detailed on the ground and are to be used for controls, then perhaps extra map detail may be requested in those areas for a specific championship contest. The first stage is to prepare a base map.

At the beginning of the year, the mappers collect all their base map information, aerial photographs and forestry maps and programme of forestry work due in the area. They divide up the area and each team member does a survey of his allocated section of the forest. Eventually, all the surveys are correlated and entered onto the base map. When this is complete after many hours of hard work and measurements, the map is drawn on sheets of drafting film. All symbols and features in Blue are drawn in the exact positions. The same is done for Brown signs, Yellow signs and features in Black.

Each colour is drawn on a separate piece of plastic film rather like tracing paper. These, of course, all have to be accurately registered from the exact overlap, and corner marks are included for the printer to use. The printer's plates are then produced and each colour register is printed on top of the others until the whole map is built up together with the key of symbols. The Controller must be allowed to check the map before it goes to the printers.

Time judges

Organisation. From now on the organiser is reasonably confident that the event will be a success because he has a Setter to put the controls in the correct places on the ground and on the new map. This is the main thing that counts to ensure the competitors' enjoyment, but make sure you have a deputy in case you are ill. Publicity must be in the front of the organiser's mind using the orienteering magazines and, if possible, advance articles in the local press. Occasionally local radio and TV can be interested in this fast-growing sport.

Equipment must be booked and collected to provide for the Setter. So an adequate number of control flags, clipper punches, and huge balls of twine must be made available.

Try to think logically through the stations of the event and note the equipment and staff needed. Your thoughts should follow this sort of line, i.e. when checking **your own organising**.

Parking. One official will need a danger notice, or flag, parking notices and should direct traffic safely. At the start of the day, he should mark traffic routes from the main roads to the event.

Preferably orienteering Orange/White signs should be placed at intervals on trees, telegraph poles and lamp posts. Remember to seek permission from the Town Clerk and the Police before you put up signs in the road. Inform the Police about the potential traffic problems at least a month in advance. Borrow road signs from Public Works Departments if they will let you, e.g. DANGER, SLOW, etc.

Make sure your registration point is close to the parking area. This can be any building such as a school, a barn, old croft or just a car or tent. Appoint a Registration Officer who will deal with all postal entries. He will post advance information, send individual start times, collect entry fees, etc., from competitors who enter in advance. There are always late entries however much they are discouraged and hence he must prepare a system to deal with unknown numbers of late arrivals. Have all the Control Cards printed to make sure they aid the administration. Separate colours for all age groups must be available for Control Cards. Never attempt to combine two age groups on one colour set, this will avoid the problem of left out ages, confusing information and so on.

D. Stewart might be David or Diane when you are trying to sort out the cards.

The Organiser can now rely on the Registrar to process the entries. He should also be able to present the final account with details of P.O.'s, cheques, etc. On the day he will need at least two assistants to take late entries and their money, so ask him to provide a float and suitable small change. They will need tables and chairs and overhead covers and, of course, a large **Registration** notice.

Prestart. The names will be called from the start list, that needs one official with a chair and perhaps a megaphone.

A finish

A start

A roped enclosure looks good but is heavy to erect, much better to buy coloured nylon twine or tapes and use light stakes of thin iron.

This will all need to be done on the day before the race, so appoint an official in charge of the whole pre-start. At least one large tent will be essential for protecting officials and the maps and course descriptions to be given out at that point. Again chairs, tables and stationery will be required at this position. A large clock or a time chart MUST be on view and this must be synchronised with the start and finish clocks.

The Starter will need a whistle and a chair and also a shelter from the weather. He may well require a relief man or a messenger.

Between the call-over of the Prestart and the actual Start line there will be about four officials on the day. They will check whistles, collect the 'stubs', give out the maps, description sheets and marshal the competitors, especially novices. A messenger will be **essential** to transport the 'stubs' to the finish every 15 or 20 minutes. Delegate one person in charge of the Prestart team and arrange, too, that it is his job to bring the **blank** maps and description sheets to the Prestart on the Sunday morning.

Master Maps. A separate official must bring all the **master** map copies and must lay out the drawing boards or tables in a proper sequence for age groups.

J.K. finish

The maps will need to be covered with an awning or at least placed under plastic covers and will need to be pinned down. Provide a set of red Biros for the younger element who forget to provide their own.

The Setter. On the penultimate day, provide him with three or four helpers merely to carry the control flags and to tie them in position at the appropriate points.

These should at least have been marked with tape so that the Controller can identify the exact positions even before the markers are placed. Although this will take place on the Saturday, the Controller and the Setter will still be obliged to run round the courses on Sunday morning to ensure that none have been removed.

Manned Controls. Ask the Setter to meet and deploy his helpers if they are going to sit near controls and check the competitors. Sometimes the second part of the mastermap may be given out halfway round the course. Quite often a time check is made at the mid-point of a competition and these helpers can be involved.

The Finish. The funnel will be erected early on race days. The ropes or coloured twine must spread **wide** to allow competitors from all directions to enter without disadvantage. After that they must narrow down to allow only a single file. The funnel at the narrow end must be long enough to enclose a lot of runners who finish at the same time and allow the officials to complete their tasks. The Control cards must be collected and the finish time entered on each. In a busy finish the competitors can either be handed a numbered time card or a numbered sticker is attached to the Control card, cards are collected and placed in order together with simultaneous finish times. On top of each batch of, say, 10 Control cards is placed a list of corresponding times. These details are later entered onto the Control cards and are passed to the score tent for processing.

Timekeepers

Score Tent. The 'stubs' have arrived already from the start and these are matched up with the Control cards as they arrive at the finish. They can be stapled or crossed out to indicate their matching. **Thus remaining stubs could eventually indicate lost persons.** The clipper indication marks must be checked and this tent must be provided with stationery and office materials. The best way for checking is to provide several giant master Control cards so that the actual competitors' cards can be placed in the centre and all marks quickly tallied.

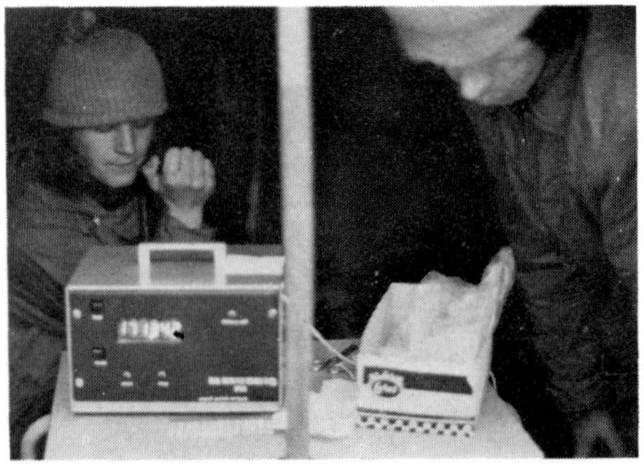

▲
Sophisticated digital timing clock with memory bank

The results should be recorded and presented from this tent on the same day as the contest.

Results Ladder. A score ladder should be erected at a suitable distance from the finish. As the results appear they have to replace earlier ones and the ladder gives an easy method for inserting names without moving lots of results.

Rope the area off to allow the officials to get access without being impeded by the spectators as seen below (see p. 17).

Results ▼

Refreshment. Free orange juice is now a tradition at even the smallest event and this is an added attraction to get people together at the Score Ladder. Remember the litter problem and provide suitable rubbish bins for the disposable cups. A large milk churn with a tap welded to the base is an ideal way of dispensing juice.

The finish and refreshments should really be sited in as scenic and sheltered a position as possible, to allow people to enjoy watching the remainder of the race in comfort and in beautiful surroundings. The prizes can then be presented in front of a sizeable audience whilst they are still eating their sandwiches.

Results. Get these to the newspapers as soon as possible, and remember to ask competitors for stamped addressed envelopes in the pre-event details sheet.

Finally, write and thank the farmer, the landowner, and all your helpers and they might all be willing to help in another year.

First Aid. It is essential that Red Cross, St. John's Ambulance or the Mountain Rescue are present at large events. The nearest doctor should be consulted and his telephone number on hand for emergencies.

▲ A finish funnel

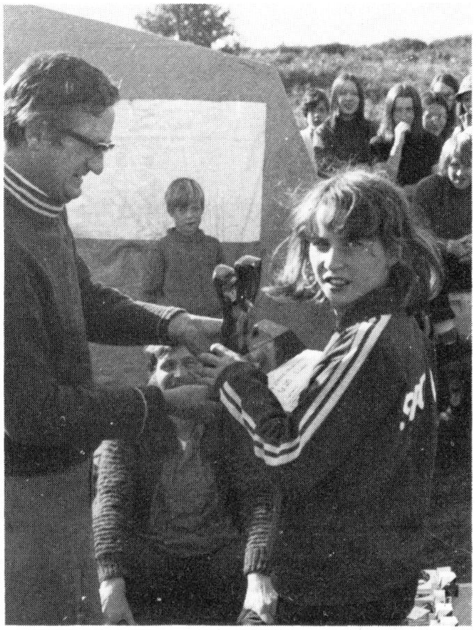

Prize giving ▶ ▼

Mountain Resue or First Aid standby

Large Event Organiser's Order List

A. Prior to Final Date for Entries

General. By this stage I am assuming that the map is made, permission for land sought, courses planned and controlled, controls premarked, initial information sheets circulated, etc.

1. Write to last year's winners for return of trophies.
2. Certificates and pennants.
3. Make out blank prize list.
4. Order Control cards and polythene bags:
   - Tape
   - Map cases
   - Pre-start, start and finish banners
   - Markers
   - Punches
   - Results ladders
   - Competitors' numbers.
5. Make out final instruction sheet.
6. Type and duplicate final instruction sheet.
7. Notices. Buy white card and directional signs.
   Make up wording for notices:
   - Those referring to registration procedures
   - Changing facilities
   - Feeding arrangements
   - Results
   - Out of bounds
   - Instructions for equipment left at start
   - Pre-start procedure
   - Map corrections
   - Start procedure
   - Master map areas
   - Anti-litter signs.
8. Type, duplicate description sheets.
9. Acquire office equipment—pens, pencils, millboards, clips, felt markers, sellotape, masking tape, staples and stapler, large envelopes, cash box, clocks and watches, typewriters, duplicators, stencils, paper, scissors, safety pins (if competitor bibs are not used), Gestetner ink, correcting fluid.
10. Sales materials, maps, pens, map cases, map books, etc.
11. Acquire equipment for hire, whistles, compasses.
12. Equipment for start and pre-start, polythene bags for clothing, a roll of small white stickers for Control cards, tapes, fence posts, etc., description sheet dispenser.
    Card spikes pre-marked + 1-15, + 16-30, etc.
    Megaphone, whistle.
    Equipment at master map areas, large hardboard sheets leaving enough room for master map and firm surface for competition map. Large polythene sheets for weather protection for master map area.
13. Finish equipment.
    Separate instruction sheets for each official detailing his specific task.
    Cards (2 sets) marked A 1-10, B 1-10, etc.
    (Time and Number Sheets.)
    Spikes—half marked with names of courses, half left blank.
14. Prepare master maps—four copies at least per course.
15. Receipt book sheet for entries received.
16. Arrange for Red Cross Team and availability of doctor.

B. After Final Date for Entries

1. Prepare start lists.
2. Make up numbered stickers.
3. Make out Control cards.
4. Make up large envelopes for larger groups, containing:
   - a. Maps.
   - b. Competitors' numbers or bibs.
   - c. Safety pins if necessary.
   - d. Control cards **both** parts completed.

e. Final instruction sheets, unless they have been sent out with notification of start times.

f. Route map from registration to start.
On the outside of envelope, write what is put into each envelope, including competition numbers or bibs and Control cards. In this way, each envelope can be double checked.

Notes of underpaid fees will be written on outside of envelope in large writing.

5. Prepare team results sheets.

6. Prepare master sheet of start times for all courses.

7. Prepare control markers with code clearly marked and punches fixed and map showing position and description of marker for control officials.

8. Make out several sets of correct sequence cards for each course—on card bigger than Control Card so that Control Cards can quickly be placed on top and sequences matched up all round card at a glance.

Each one should be clearly marked with name of course and Control Card colour.

9. Check with caterer a final number for meals for competitors and officials.

10. Check First Aid arrangements and availability of doctor.

11. Double check all map corrections, master maps, code letters on control markers and description sheets, control sequence cards. Then recheck them all again.

12. Double check that you have all equipment you require.

13. See separate sheet for officials required and their duties, etc., plus control official sheets for competitors times and numbers. Recheck availability of all officials. Notify them of task and time and place to report to.

14. Arrange for transportation of all necessary furniture and heavy equipment.

C. **Day prior to Competition**

1. Set out controls in forest.
2. Arrange furniture, etc.
3. Tape route from final control(s) to finish. Tape route to start, and start to master map areas.
4. If using a building set up furniture, notices, etc., for registration, finish and results, changing facilities, etc.
5. Arrange boxes of small equipment for Start officials, Finish officials, including spare Control Cards, registration officials.
6. Set up tents, etc., for prestart, start and finish.
7. Make up specific instruction sheets for each official.

D. **Day of Competition**

1. Arrange for control officials to be put in position. SYNCHRONISE WATCHES OF ALL OFFICIALS.
2. Mark route to start and route signs on approach roads.
3. Lay out start area and prestart area.
4. Lay out master map area.
5. Lay out finish system and results system.
6. Check registration system. Separate table for large groups pre-entered for distribution of envelopes containing all required. Separate table for each class with supplies of bibs, maps, safety pins, instruction sheets, Control Cards, spare cash, receipt books and start list showing blanks.

7. Lay out map corrections on tables well marked.

8. Brief all officials in groups, registration, prestart, start, finish, results, etc.

9. Stage complete run through of registration, start and finish procedures.
   KEEP ALL COMPETITORS, SPECTATORS, etc., WELL AWAY FROM FINISH AND RESULTS OFFICIALS.

   LEAVE YOURSELF AND CHIEF REGISTRATION, START AND FINISH OFFICIALS CLEAR OF SPECIFIC TASKS TO ENABLE THEM TO SUPERVISE AND ANSWER QUERIES.

E. After Completion of Competition

1. Arrange for clearing of all sites.
2. Information to press.
3. Letters of thanks.
4. Publication of results (including rescrutiny of cards).
5. Return of all equipment borrowed.
6. Complete post-event forms and B.O.F. form C1.
7. Donations to Red Cross, rescue organisations.
8. Payment of bills and statement of accounts (including B.O.F. levy).

The Badge Scheme

The B.O.F. has recently approved a new scheme for proficiency awards. The two main innovations are a new Championship badge and the introduction of gold standard awards for all classes.

The Championship Badge

This is an annual award, inaugurated in 1971 after the British Championships. It is open to any orienteer who, in the preceding year, has achieved better than the winner's time in his/her class plus 25% in three of the following events:

1. The British Senior and Intermediate Championships.
2. The British Junior Championships.
3. The Jan Kjellstrom Individual Event.
4. The five regional championships, i.e. Scottish, Northern, Midlands, Southern and the South-Western Championships.

A qualifying time must be achieved in at least one of the events in 1–3. The badge is not generally available for 'B' classes nor may a qualifying time achieved in one class count towards a badge in another class.

The National Badge Scheme

Badges will be awarded on the results of National Events (those which appear in capitals in the fixture list). The scheme is open to all orienteers (except Wayfinders) who compete on their own and reach the required standard in three events.

GOLD	Better than the average of the first three competitors' times plus 25%.
SILVER	Better than the average of the first three competitors' times plus 50%.
BRONZE	Better than the average of the first three competitors' times plus 100%.
IRON	Successful completion of the course.

These standards now apply to all classes with the exception of **all** 'B' classes, where Silver standard becomes plus 25% and bronze plus 50%.
Should there be less than 20 competitors in a class the average of the first two only is taken. If there are less than ten the winner's time alone is used for the calculation of the standards. At the controller's discretion the badge scheme may not apply in certain small classes where no competitor has achieved a satisfactory time.

Initially, competitors are restricted to obtaining their badges in their own class. But holders of a Boys/Girls Gold award may compete in a Junior class and likewise holders of a Junior gold may compete in Intermediate classes and holders of an Intermediate gold may compete in Senior classes. The present age limits of the classes means that there is a time limit of three years for obtaining a badge; this will also apply in senior classes.

Applicants for badges should indicate which of the following alternatives they wish to receive:

a. Brooch badge and certificate

b. Cloth badge and certificate

c. All three

The certificate measures $8\frac{1}{2}'' \times 11''$ so please send a suitable envelope if you do not wish it to be folded.

The Environment and the Fringe

Golden eagle

In Scotland the forests are nearly always coniferous but sometimes they are the more picturesque beech plantations or other deciduous species such as oak or silver birch.

For the survival of the sport the environment must not be spoiled and anyone that says 300 runners will damage a forest obviously does not understand the sport. The beauty of it is that nearly every competitor chooses a different route and so each area only has a few passers-by. In large Scandinavian events the forests easily swallow up literally thousands of orienteers. In 1975 the 5-day 'O'-Ringen meeting had over 10,000 entrants from over 15 nations.

More of the forest fauna will be seen during training events due to the lower density of people intruding upon the respective habitats. Deer are only dangerous during the rutting season, but care should be taken if you accidentally come across a red deer that may not be aware of you.

Now where is that control flag?

The swift orienteering expert will have little time to look out for animal life but his quiet progress may well startle a deer or surprise a squirrel or a hare. The young competitor or the middle-aged may be quite content to indulge his interest in the sport and in nature simultaneously. When competitors are moving about a forest in all directions it is not surprising that a retreat by an animal from one human may well bring him in your direction.

In some of the forests deer are so plentiful that one constantly hears them scatter in the undergrowth after a noisy approach. The smaller roe deer are adept at making themselves scarce but under the circumstances of competitions they are frequently observed.

The author once visited a control 'on the stream' and was surprised to see a roe deer buck happily drinking only 10 feet away. The red deer, however, would need to be avoided if you accidentally came close to his cover.

The fallow deer is uncommon but is included here merely to satisfy curiosity and to aid identification. The deer have no incisor teeth on the top jaw, but they are replaced by a horny pad, and hence when twigs are bitten only the bottom edge is clear cut, and the top is torn. So the trees are damaged, particularly at the very young stage, by the activities of deer in their grazing, browsing and fraying. The latter means rubbing their antlers on tree trunks.

Roe are grey brown in winter but turn russet red in the summer and only the buck has antlers. If you surprise these deer in the undergrowth they may well emit sharp staccato barks as they rush away. You will notice the effect of earlier damage to trees when you come across small clearings deep in the forest and often the trees are stunted with leafy bushy trunks. Norway spruce is susceptible but the prickly spines of the sitka spruce tend to save it from browsing roe deer.

Fallow deer stag

Mapping

When permission and decisions have been finalised about the area to be mapped, the mapper will need to obtain every scrap of information that he can lay his hands on relating to the forest.

He can easily obtain the 1 inch and $2\frac{1}{2}$ inch series of the forest, with luck there might be a 6 inch map covering his area. Usually maps concentrate on urban detail and the communicating systems of roads, they tend to neglect the fine details of 'wilderness' areas. One can hardly expect the surveyor to worry too much about the dimensions of a depression a mile inside a dense forest on the side of a steep hill. However, orienteers do care and thus their details tend to be better **inside** the forest.

The forester may provide a photo copy of original plantings of trees, which might include old roads, tracks, and ruins that are now overgrown and forgotten. Mappers often try to get aerial photos from the appropriate Government department and of course these are invaluable as a proper **base** for a map. The correct shape, width and length can be accurately checked. The line features such as roads, streams, walls and fences can be copied accurately and even the contour levels can be indicated. Remember that they sometimes cause errors if the feature is completely covered from the air by overgrowing trees.

Although much laborious legwork is alleviated a good deal of ground checking must be undertaken to avoid errors.

All of the information can now be placed tentatively on tracing paper or plastic mapping film. If aerial photos are absent all line features on the O.S. maps must be accurately paced or better still chained. It is not difficult to construct a measuring wheel for difficult and hilly terrain, it is certainly incomparable for accuracy.

So at last a **Base** map is constructed onto which all other features can be plotted. Mappers tend to delegate sections of the forest to members of the team.

Each man will then take cross bearings from accurately surveyed reference points and will pace distances connecting each feature.

This information will be given in note form to the chief mapper who will later transfer all of the information to his base map. He will need to be a careful draughtsman and apply the scale to all the measurements that he has been given.

After **many** hours of very patient work a final map will have been drawn, some areas may have to be rechecked but at least every feature has been found and surveyed. Please never criticise a map unless you have personally made one and you know how much work is involved!

Printing

To produce a 4-colour map it is necessary to provide the printer with four separate accurately matched tracings of the four sets of coloured marks. Register marks for alignment must be provided on each tracing.

Tracing No. 1 will look like this showing the **Yellow** clearings and fields.

Tracing No. 2 will only show the **Blue** rivers, streams, ponds, sea, marshes, etc. It may also show, as here, the Magnetic North lines.

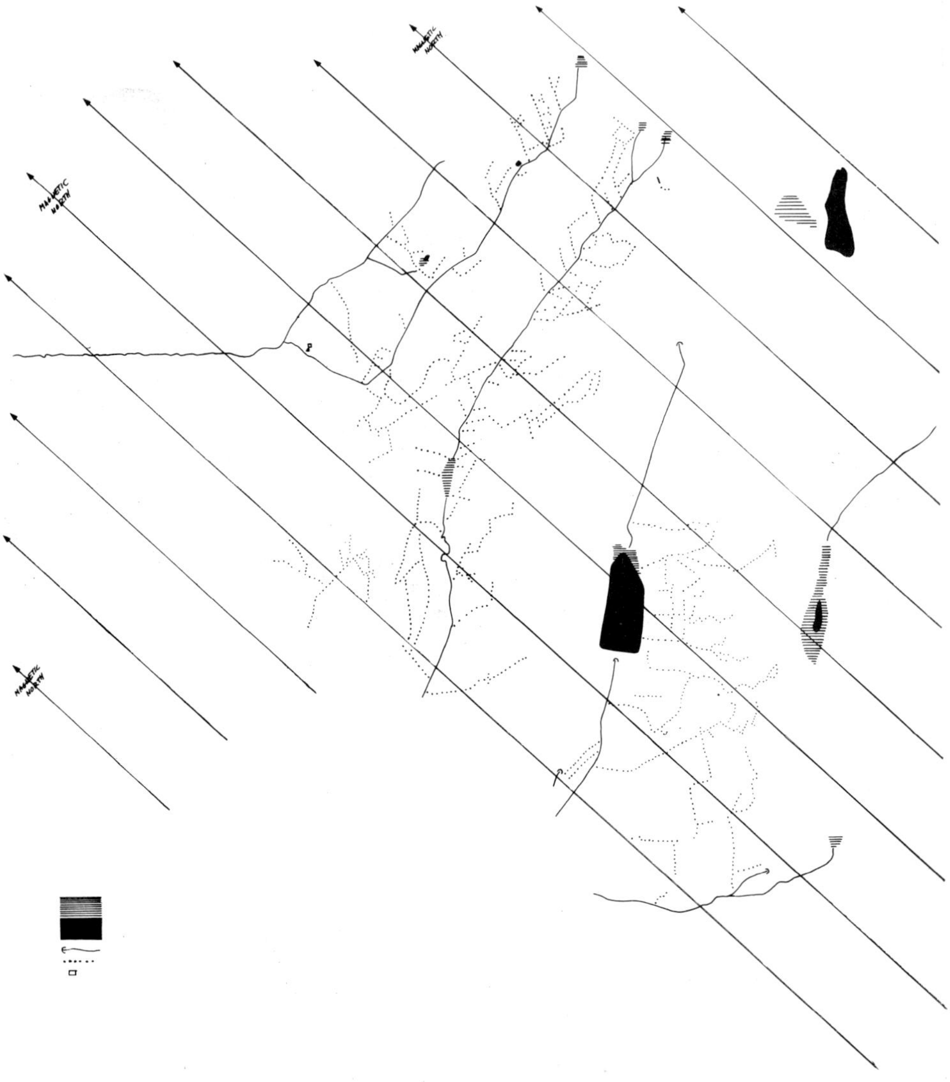

Tracing No. 3 will have the **Black** features like roads, tracks, paths, walls, fences, boulders, towers, boundaries, and electric power lines. Some word Keys apply to the Brown, Yellow or Blue symbols.

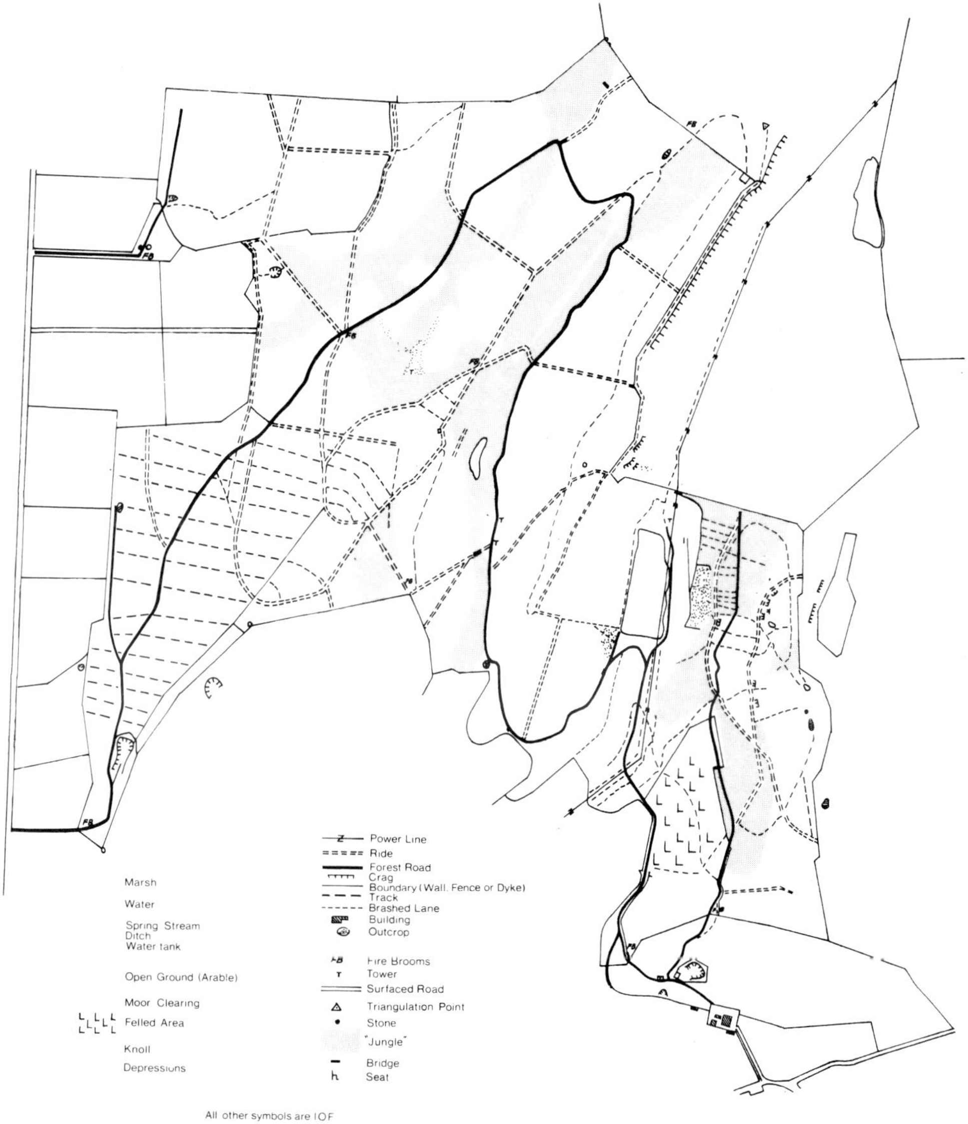

Tracing No. 4 for the **Brown** contours, depressions, knolls and wooded marshes.

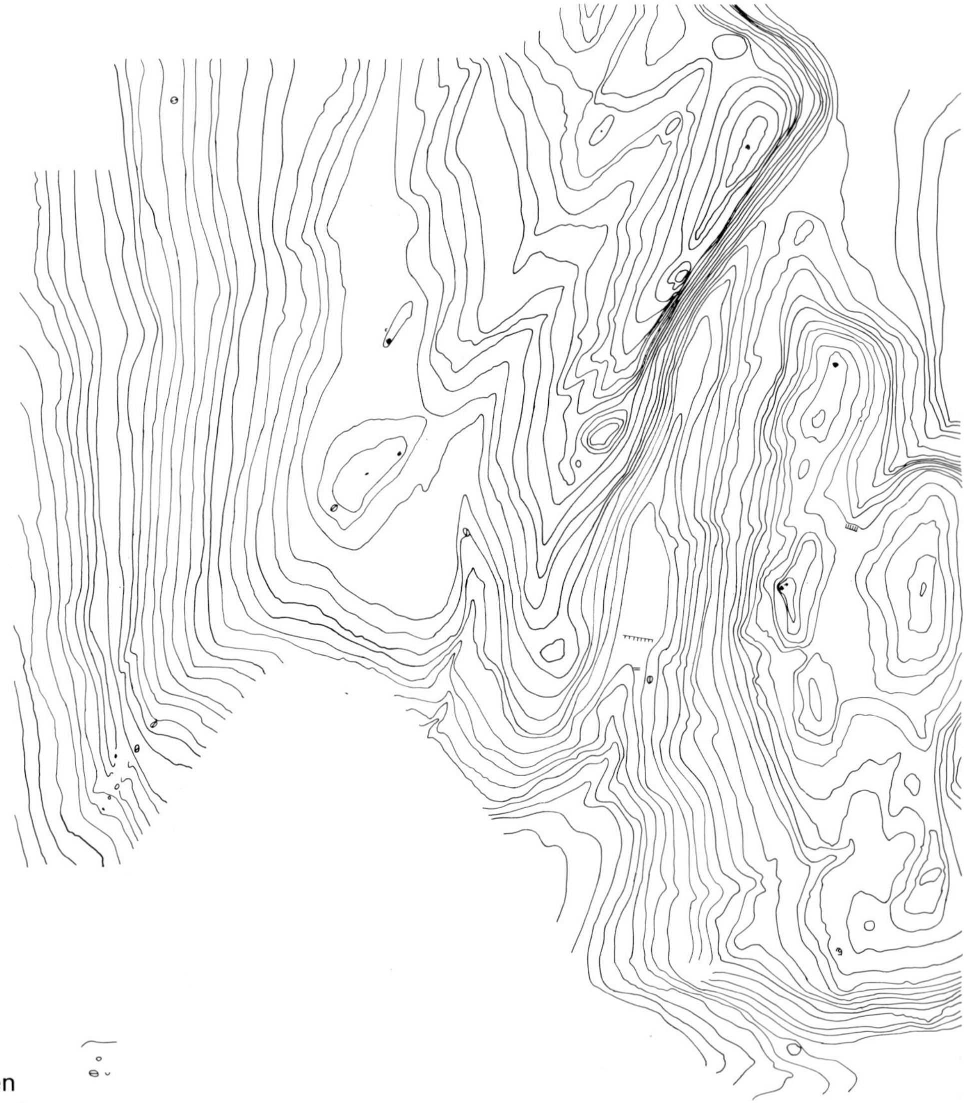

If a description of the map symbols is also to be printed then of course the appropriate coloured symbols must also be added to the tracing separations.

Hallyburton Forest shows how the sport evolved in earlier years

The tracings are photographed and then an etched plate is made for each colour separation. When the paper is placed in the press it must be carefully aligned and thus a register mark or cross is placed at each corner so that each printing run can be properly aligned.

Then the paper goes through the press and the Brown sheet might be done first. The paper is returned and run through again, this time with the next litho plate to give the Yellow register. After that the paper is run through two more times to have the Black and Blue parts of the map overprinted.

If the control markers and the courses are to be indicated a fifth printing in Red ink will be required to obtain an overprinted map. This would alleviate the need for master maps in the case of a mass start score event or a large championship.

The final map of Hallyburton Forest may be seen on p. 119.
All of this is expensive and permanent so a map must be justified before being embarked upon.
Ideally the map, not an event, should be the primary consideration, though events can then, of course, be set using the map made. A situation in which event deadline dates are imposed on the map-making should be avoided if possible.

Hallyburton Forest is on the road between Dundee and Coupar Angus in Scotland, and the farm at the South of the map is known as Tullybaccart Farm. Why not visit this forest and try to follow the routes and recognise the photos taken of the actual terrain?
Your local forest can be treated in the same way to produce a reasonable map.
In 1967 a P.E. Lecturer, Mr. I. Brown, decided to start an orienteering club. He worked at Dundee University and called out a few students to try the sport. Since there were no maps he could only use the $2\frac{1}{2}$ in. black and white O.S. version. (Map A.)

This was adequate for a lot of enjoyment. Following on in 1971 the students tried a new map which they drew for themselves. It was not special but at least it had the orienteering symbols instead of the O.S. signs. Several orienteering events were arranged and despite comments about the accuracy of the map a lot of people became interested in the new sport. (Map B)

Map C was drawn. This was far more detailed as so many orienteers had quartered the forest looking for identifiable features.
In 1972, when it was drawn, it was a very fair effort although the actual neatness of the drawing

Hallyburton Forest

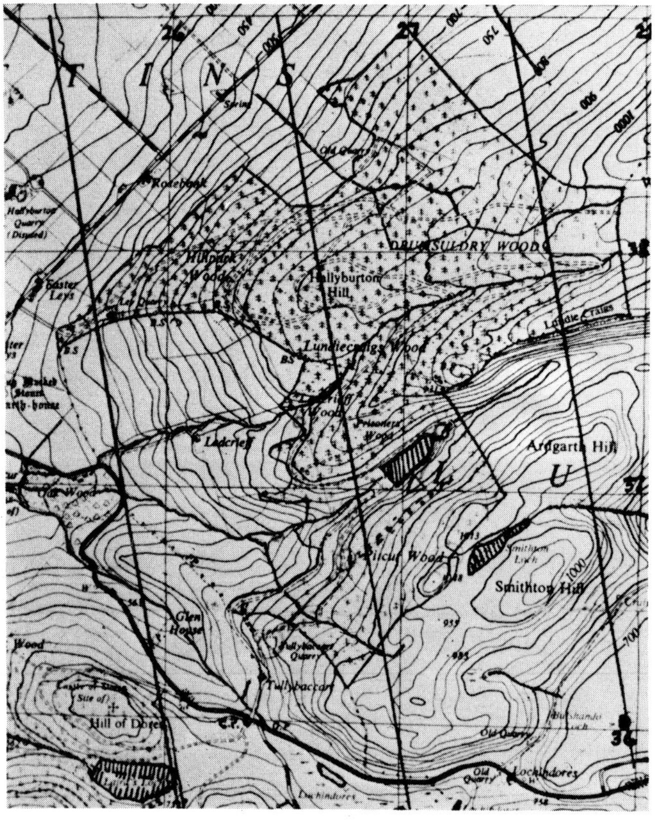

▲ Map A

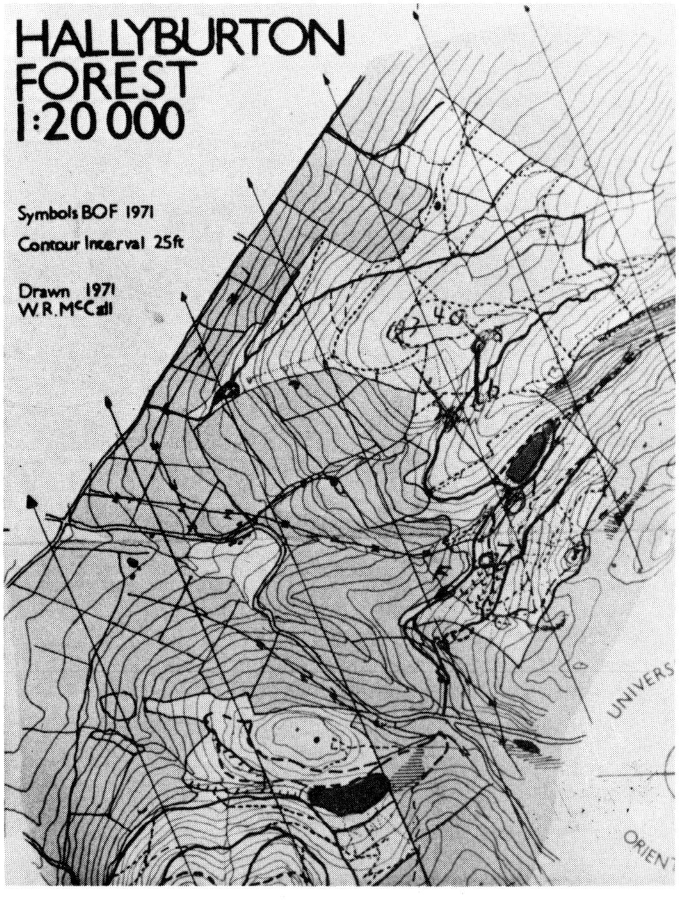

Map B ▶

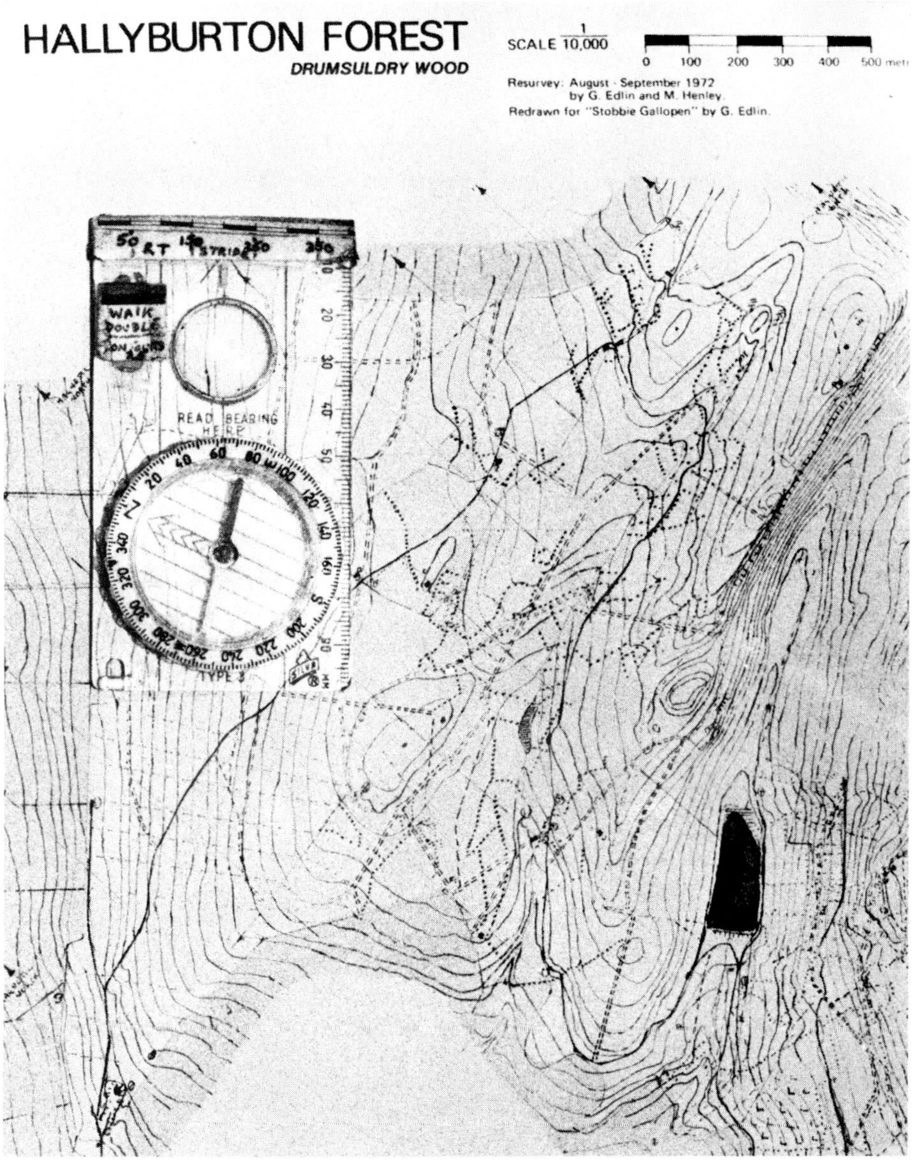

◀ Map C

was criticised. Some features in pale yellow such as small clearings were almost impossible to see and some fence boundaries were too thinly printed, so too were the magnetic North lines.

In the next two years several new features were found and some tree felling took place. However, the next stage, now that the sport has developed sufficiently to provide adequate volunteers, will allow for a really top class map. The point is that now the area has built up a club the schools are actively taking part, and also the University is keen. This is how your own area may need to develop before an expensive and laborious map appears. Maps can be made by single volunteers who are experienced, and this has been found to be far more efficient than teams of mappers. In addition, this slow development on various grades of maps has provided numbers of potential course setters. So don't be afraid to try your hand at embryonic maps, they can always be used for training purposes or for gathering information **prior** to the production of a top grade map suitable for a Badge or Championship event.

Try to identify all the Control points and actual photos on the map on p. 119 of **Hallyburton Forest** as used for an actual event. Using the map try to estimate the position and direction that the photos were taken from.

Car parking was available in the quarry and thus Pre-start was placed just inside the forest boundary on the farm track grass verge.

The start is shown and the **Master maps** were placed out of sight up the slope indicated by the Red triangle. The **first** Control was **The Summit** and was placed far away to spread out the starters and to give plenty of route choices even though the summit was visible.

The best route is shown, where the competitor takes an almost straight line along the wall and follows tracks and ditches all the way. Any attempt to travel across the clearing meets with tree trunks and difficult bracken and thorns (photo A). The summit has a fine Cairn on the top, while the beautiful view of the River Tay 10 miles away is enough to stimulate anyone to enjoy themselves (photos B and C).

▼ The clearing

▲ Photo A

◀ The Cairn (Photo B)

▲ The summit—control No 1

View from the summit (Photo C)
▼

▼ The crag—control No 2

D

Above: The stream is strewn with obstacles (E)

Control 2. The Crag (above). This was difficult but refreshing after the previous uphill fight. The ditches present quick travel as the trees are so thick and the undergrowth is very dense.

Control 3. The Well. Now the competitor takes a ditch and runs directly towards the loch which does not need compass work. If he approaches from the South it is a mistake as the stream has such steep banks and is strewn with obstacles (above right). Much better to take the track to the North and approach down the spur to easily see the flat covered well from above (right photo F).

The well—control No 3 ▶

Part of the spur or hillside above the well, shown only by contours

▲ G Contours!

◀ H The ruined bridge on the easy track route

▼ J

The track junction—control No 4

Control 4. The Track Junction. Everyone will make for the forest road and the unwary novice will fall into the trap of the obvious shortest straight line approach. (Photo G.) Just look at the contours of the stream valley and, in addition, the well watered undergrowth is seen on p. 65. The experienced man will tend to keep to routes which allow fast travel. His choice will be further but much faster taking him up the track to the ride, past this interesting ruined bridge (photo H) and at the end of the ride he will easily find the track junction. (Photo J.)

The tower—control No 5

K ▲

Control 5. The Tower (High Seat). The Western route will find the complications of the many ditches far too difficult whereas the Eastern approach uses the footpath and the last ditch as a direct attack point to the tower (above). (Photo K.)

Control 6. The Old Bridge. A rather boring leg that should make all but novices use the road. The novices will learn the hard way if they follow the stream to the bridge (right). (Photo L.)

The Old Bridge (L) ▶

The old bridge—control No 6

Control 7. The Knoll (below). Again there are two routes to the open moorland and there is really nothing to advantage with either of them.

The Knoll (M)—control No 7 ▼

◀ The Boundary Stone (N)—control No 8

▼ The cliff-top route (P)

Control 8. The Boundary Stone (above right). (Photo N.) This control is very small and needs extra markers around it, or bunting. The cliff route is not really dangerous, there is a well defined footpath and all competitors can easily see any potential hazard. The alternative is a footpath via the trees, which although winding, and in places overgrown, does lead almost through the control point. The cliff route (right) causes the competitor to lose time backtracking and he has only a poor attack point from the bend. Note the pylons in the valley in photo P and find them on the map.

▼ (Q) Looking towards control 9 from P

(R) Looking North to position P
▼

Control 9. The Fence Corner (above). Easy. You can see the boundary fence down there.

Funny how you missed it! Look more carefully at the precise position of the control—that crafty course setter. So go back down to the gate and find the correct fence this time! Admit it, you are getting tired and careless just as the setter expected!

The Finish. Watch out for the marshy area (above right) and sprint for home down the track to the North of the loch. This position was deliberately chosen as a beautiful site for competitors to eat their sandwiches and to watch competitors coming along the cliff route. It was easy to arrange that a few official vehicles transport refreshments, results ladder apparatus and the track suits from the start to the finish along the forest road from the car park.

Try to take photographs to illustrate the contour features and objects of interest in your local forest as they become very useful for teaching purposes.

Try also to calculate all the alternative routes possible on the Hallyburton map and practise measuring compass bearings that you might need if you were competing on this area.

Now it's your turn, so let's talk about 'O' maps, so that you can begin to make them.

In Scotland in the mid-60's photocopies of $2\frac{1}{2}$ in. maps were used. However, unlike England, there was not a complete cover of $2\frac{1}{2}$ in. North of the Highland fault line and many were 80 years old. These maps at 1:25,000 were barely adequate because so much was lost in the photocopying and so few features were shown **inside** the forests. Orienteers began to draw their own black and white maps and to add features and then to photo-reproduce copies of their own works. This meant searching in the forests for unmarked knolls, depressions, and ditches.

At the stage of 1970 most maps were still black and white but a few had been done in colour. Black was for line features, brown for contours and blue for all wet features but there was little standardisation of colour codes.

Early 'O' maps

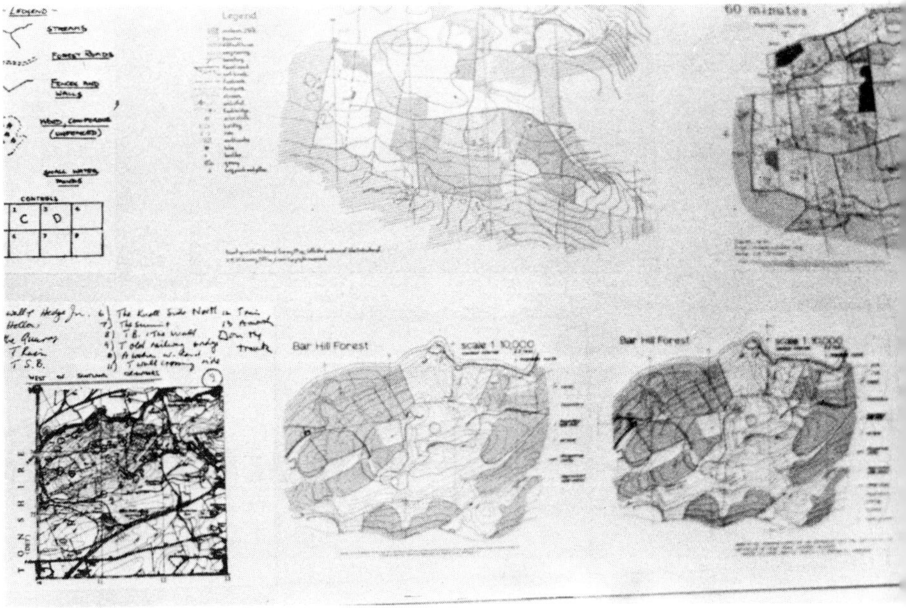

The photo shows the evolution of two sets of maps over the years, as also seen by the Hallyburton developments in the previous section, the latter having yet to be made into a first class map.

The most recent innovation is the plotting of accurate base maps directly from aerial photographs, and is called photogrammetry.

This is followed by extensive field surveying and careful draughtsmanship to produce four or five colour maps by separations as previously explained. Up to date colours are now agreed by convention as follows.

Colour code descriptions should be learnt by heart **NOW**.

Open land—yellow ochre.

Rough land—yellow and black.

Felled—yellow with L signs.

Windblown—yellow + green bars.

Runnable forest—white.

Walk (difficult)—light green.

Fight (very dense)—**dark** green.

N.B.—Yellow tapes **in** the forest mean danger, e.g. a deep quarry.

Mappers should not be without the book **Mapping** by Robin Harvey (obtainable from B.O.F.).

When you are a competent orienteer you may develop your interest by organising events, training other people or perhaps you will try setting or mapping. If there are no existing maps in your area start with a simple area in black and white. Even close to town do not rush into colour because it costs over £100, be content to provide fun for schools and clubs while gathering information. Naturally over the months extra features will be found, planting and felling can be recorded and finally the printer can be given drawings two or four times larger than the final map. He will reduce it to the proper scale and still be able to keep all the details.

Later, after a series of small events using the map and still noting criticisms and errors it will be time to justify a colour map and the high cost. Have a large number run off and take care of the printer's plates.

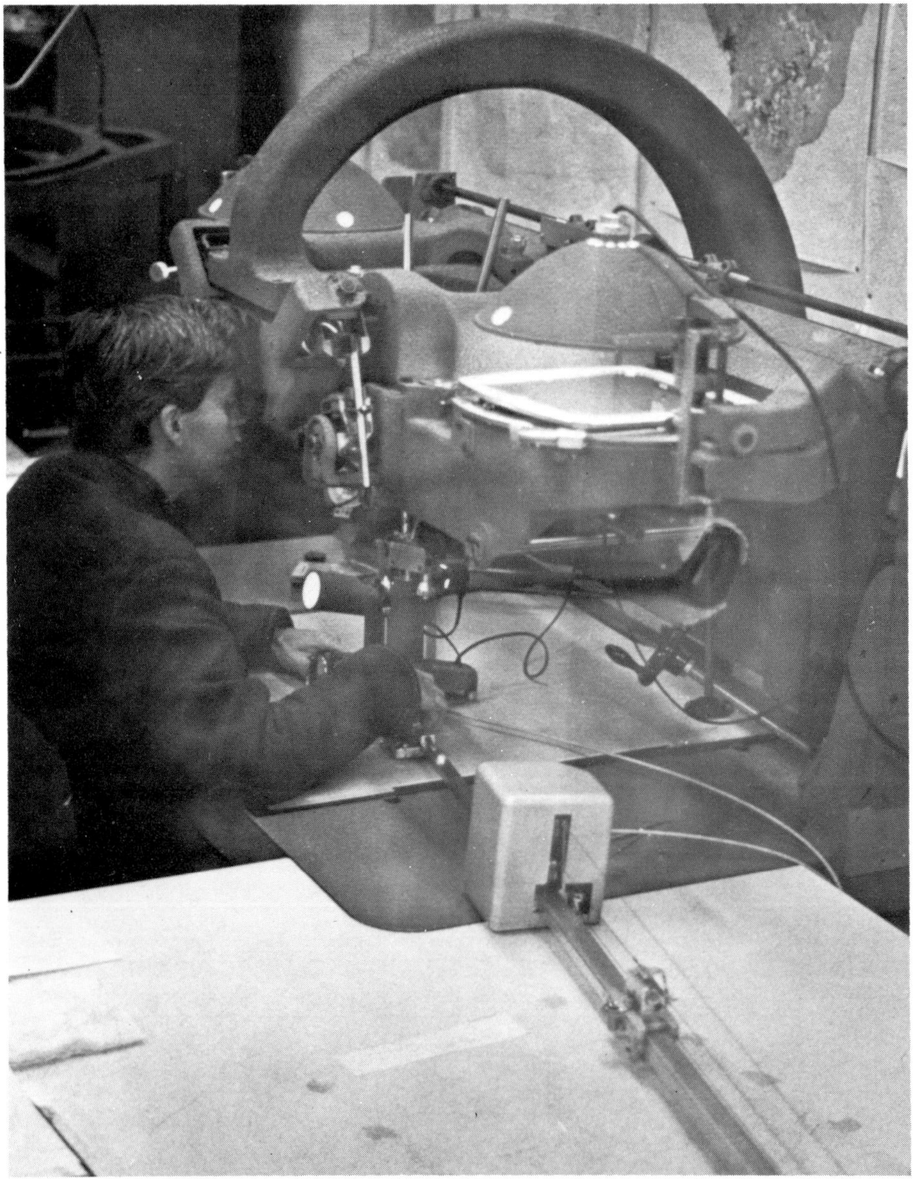

In the photo, the operator is tracing outlines with a pencil on a suitably geared armature to give the exact scale of his choosing for the final map. Contours are followed with a light spot which can be made to travel around only the areas exactly in focus and therefore at the same height.

The shortcomings of aerial photos of forests is that the place is covered in tall trees. The careful mapper must walk round the forest and record the average height of trees in each section. In the office he can adjust the plotting machine to allow for tree height when producing contours on the base map. Finally, the photogrammetry has produced a map that is correct for line features such as roads and streams and the shape of the forest. It will show all clearings and rides together with hills and valleys in contour form. The survey must record all hidden features

Scribing an 'O' map over a light table

such as knolls, small depressions and all objects shielded by trees, e.g., walls, fences, ditches, parts of the streams and ruins. These must all be located with pacing and cross-bearings from known base map features.

To produce separations for colour, special mapping pens must be used to give the exact line widths corresponding with B.O.F. symbols. The mapper draws each separation on drafting film and hands them to the printer.

Scribing is more versatile because of the ease of making either positives or negatives for the printer. You must ask your printer which type he can handle on his particular machines, before you start drawing the final map. A special scribing tool gives the various line widths and cuts into the plastic sheets or masks, showing up the lines from a 'light table'. The photo shows the mapper working late into the night using her home light table, which is essential for the expert 'O' mapper. These maps approach works of art and all aids such as Letraset for headings must be employed to set off the finished article. This also includes the use of Letratone dot screens for drafting film and various density masks to indicate 'runnability' areas when using scribing sheets.

I would like to end by voicing the appreciation of all orienteers for the excellent and selfless work done by mappers, setters and organisers, past and present, for giving them such an enjoyable sport. Thank you.

P

SYMBOLS FOR BRITISH ORIENTEERING MAPS

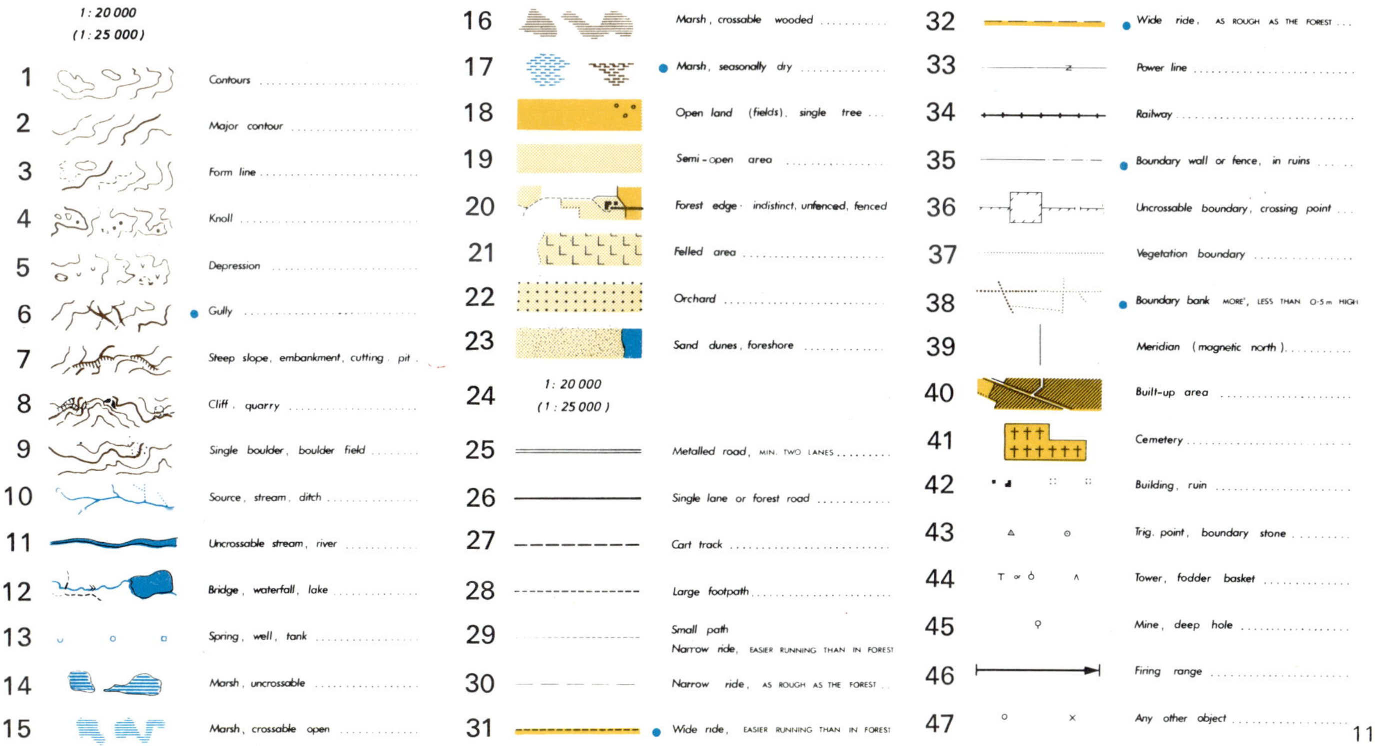

Fig. 10.

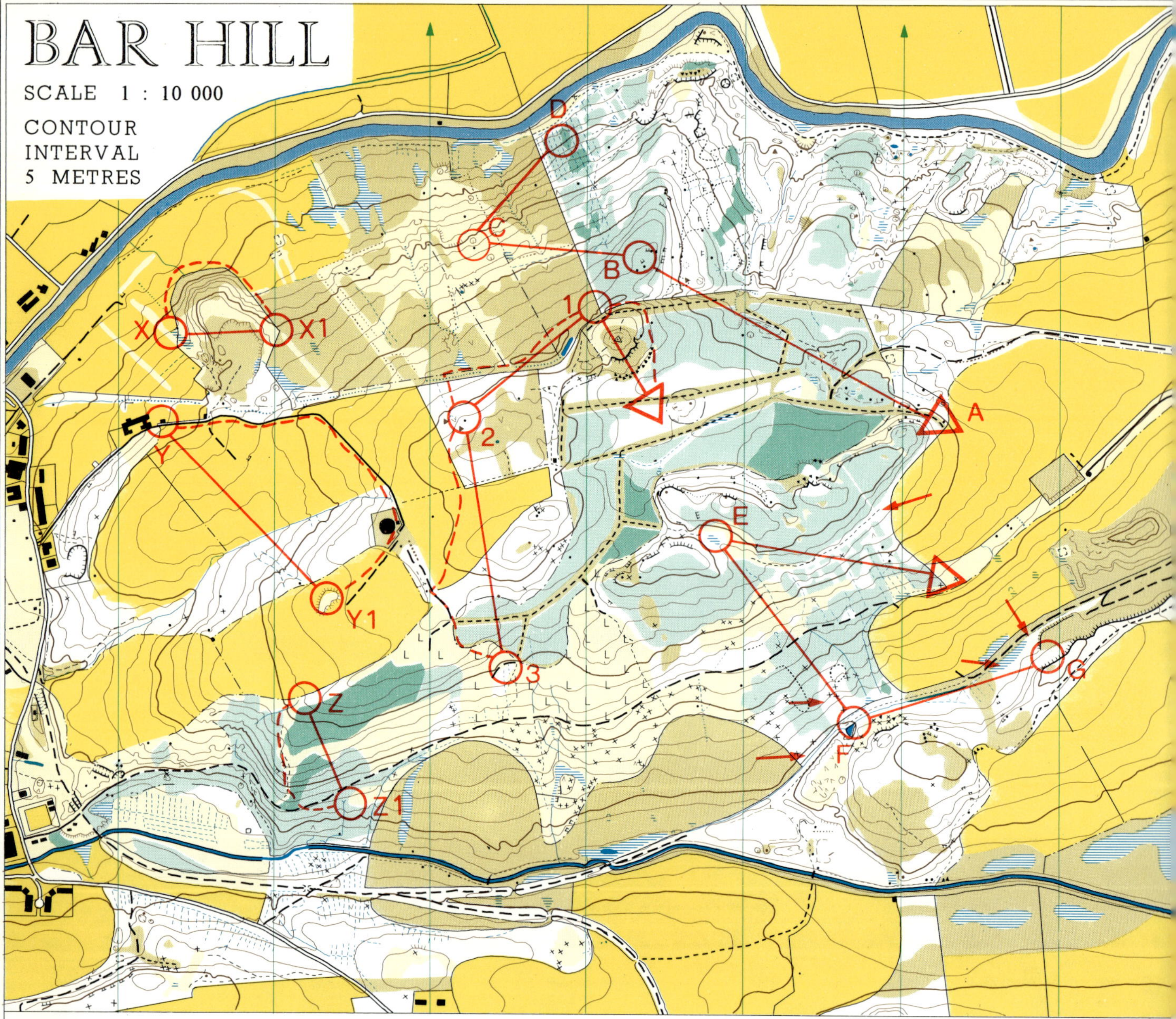

open field
open rough
semi open
platform
root stock
crag or outcrop
dangerous crag
linear marsh
0 100 200 300
METRES
cart track or dismantled railway
ditch wet or dry
dangerous water
felled
walk
fight

Photogrammetry by K. Dahl
Surveyed and drawn by J. A. T. Richards, 1973

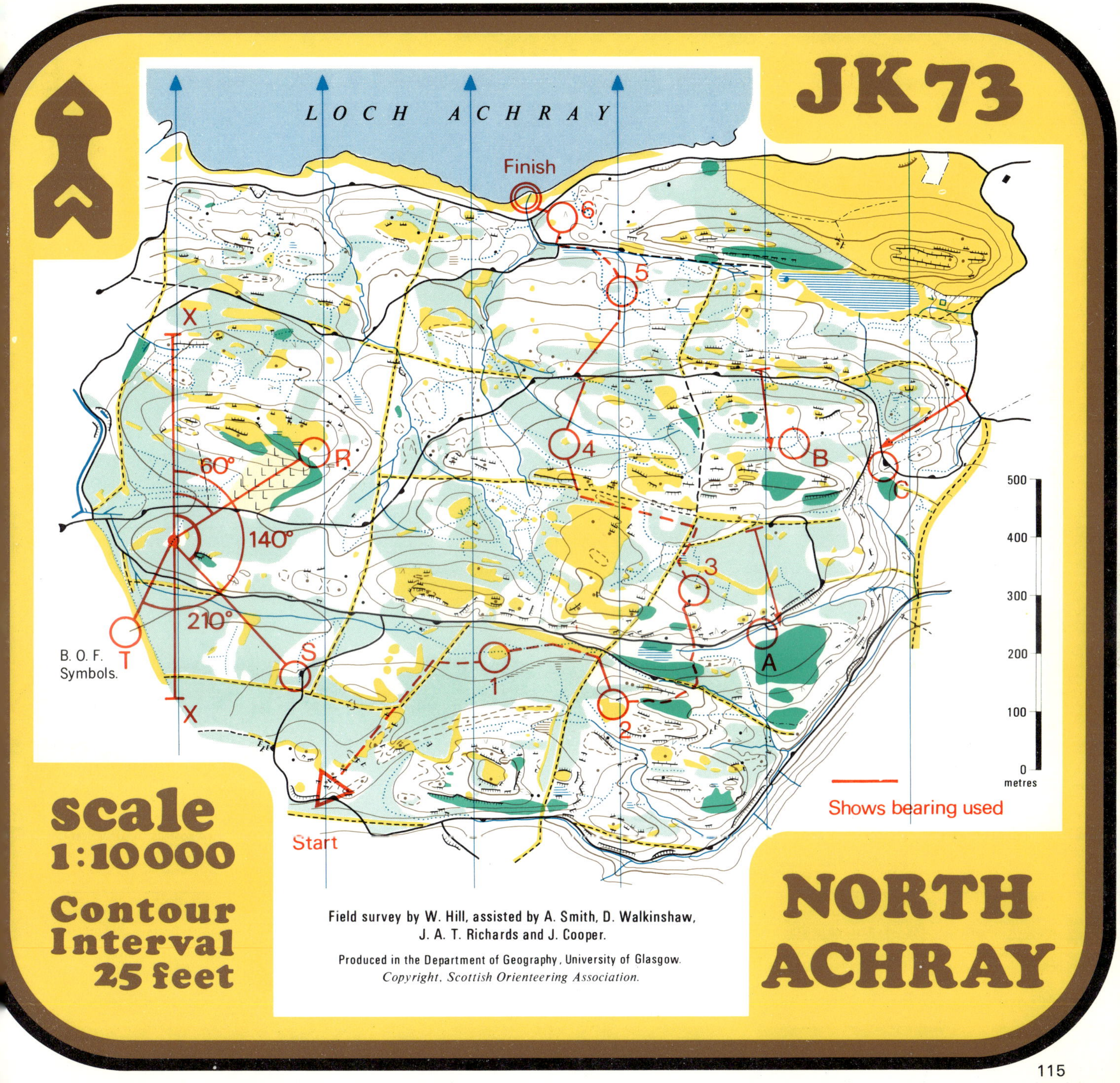
JK73
LOCH ACHRAY
Finish
Start
B. O. F. Symbols.
60°
140°
210°
Shows bearing used
500
400
300
200
100
0
metres
scale 1:10000
Contour Interval 25 feet
NORTH ACHRAY
Field survey by W. Hill, assisted by A. Smith, D. Walkinshaw, J. A. T. Richards and J. Cooper.
Produced in the Department of Geography, University of Glasgow.
Copyright. Scottish Orienteering Association.

BROWNMUI KIRKLEEG

Scale

Contour Interval

Based on the Ordn
with the sanction
Her Majesty's

Field Surv
assisted by A. Me

Dra

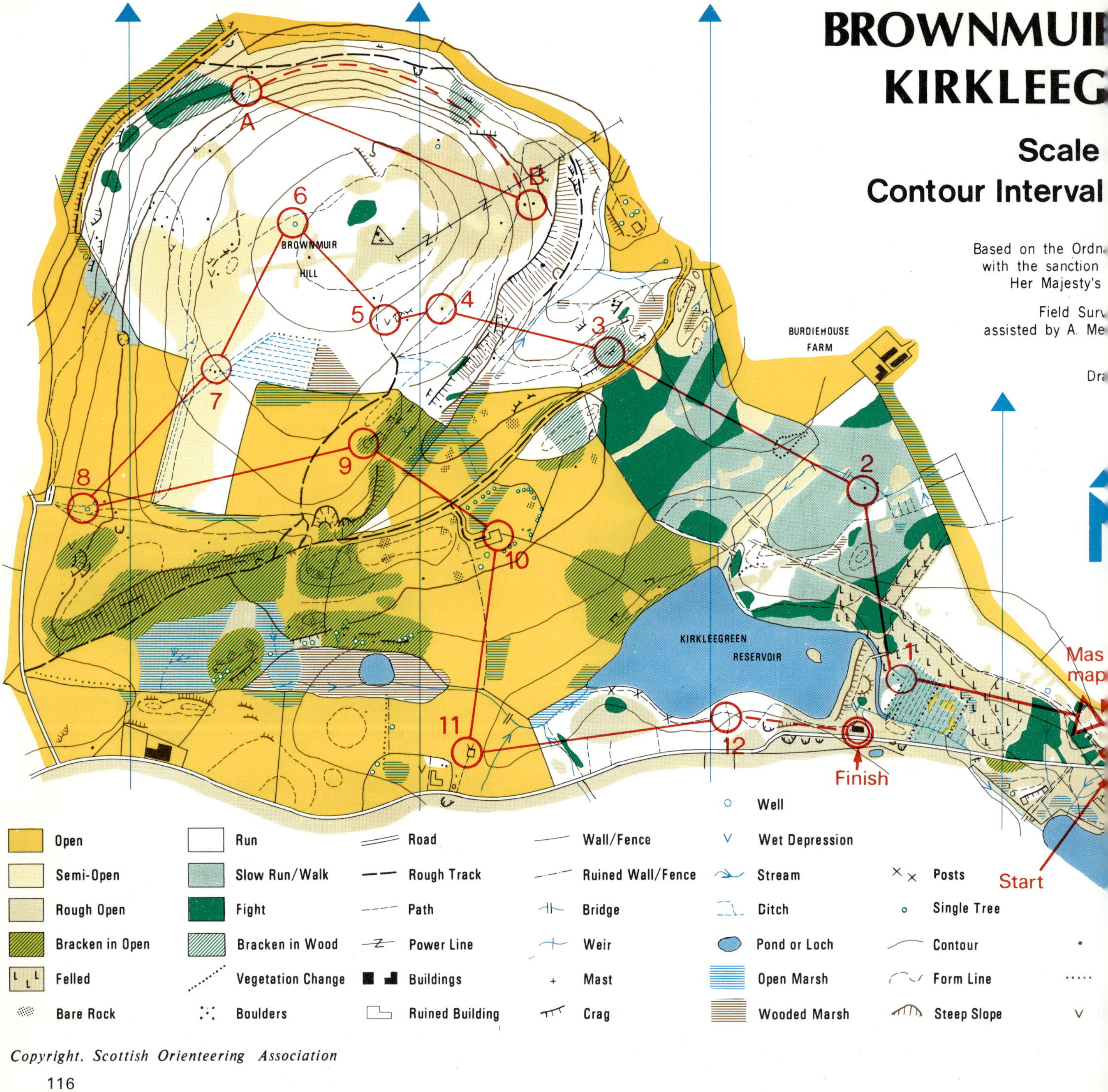

Novices Walk, Stage 1

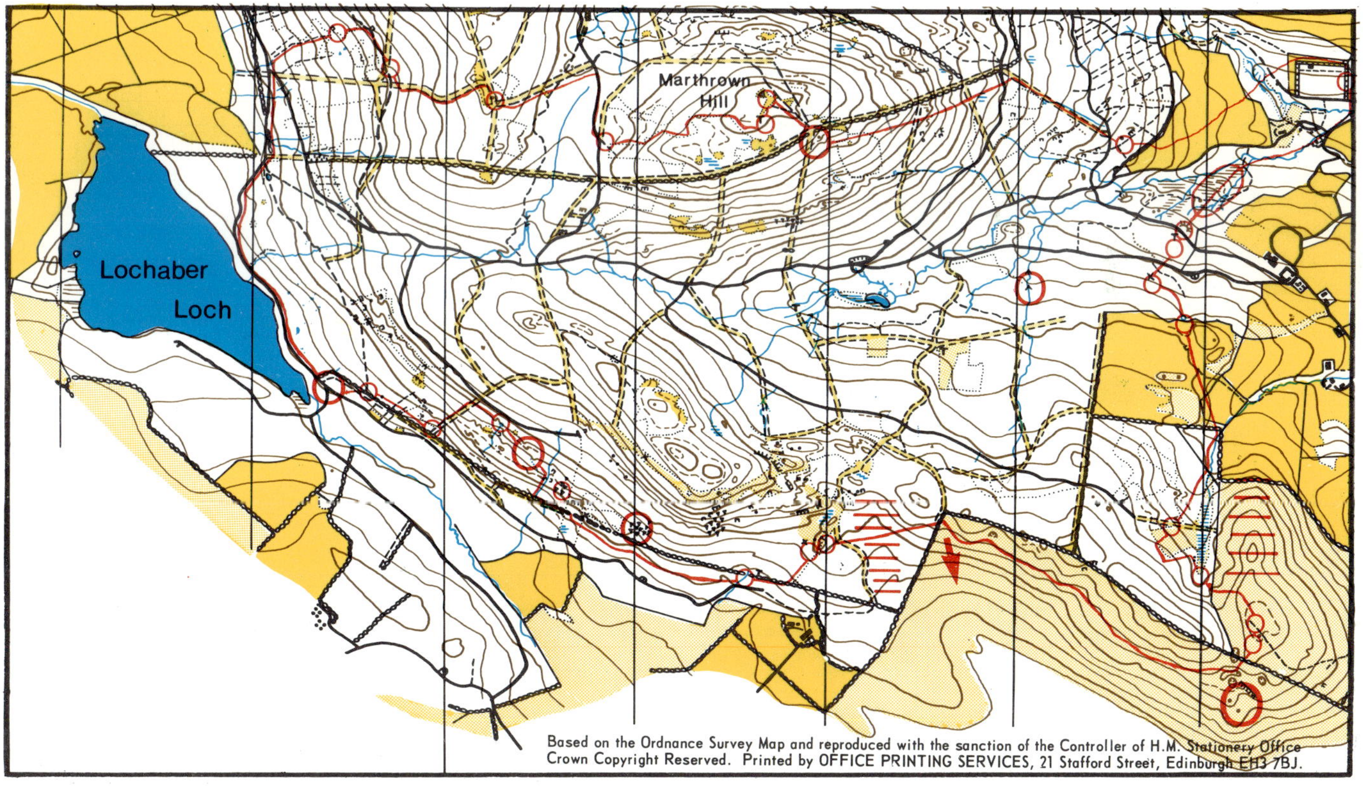

Novices Walk, Stage 2

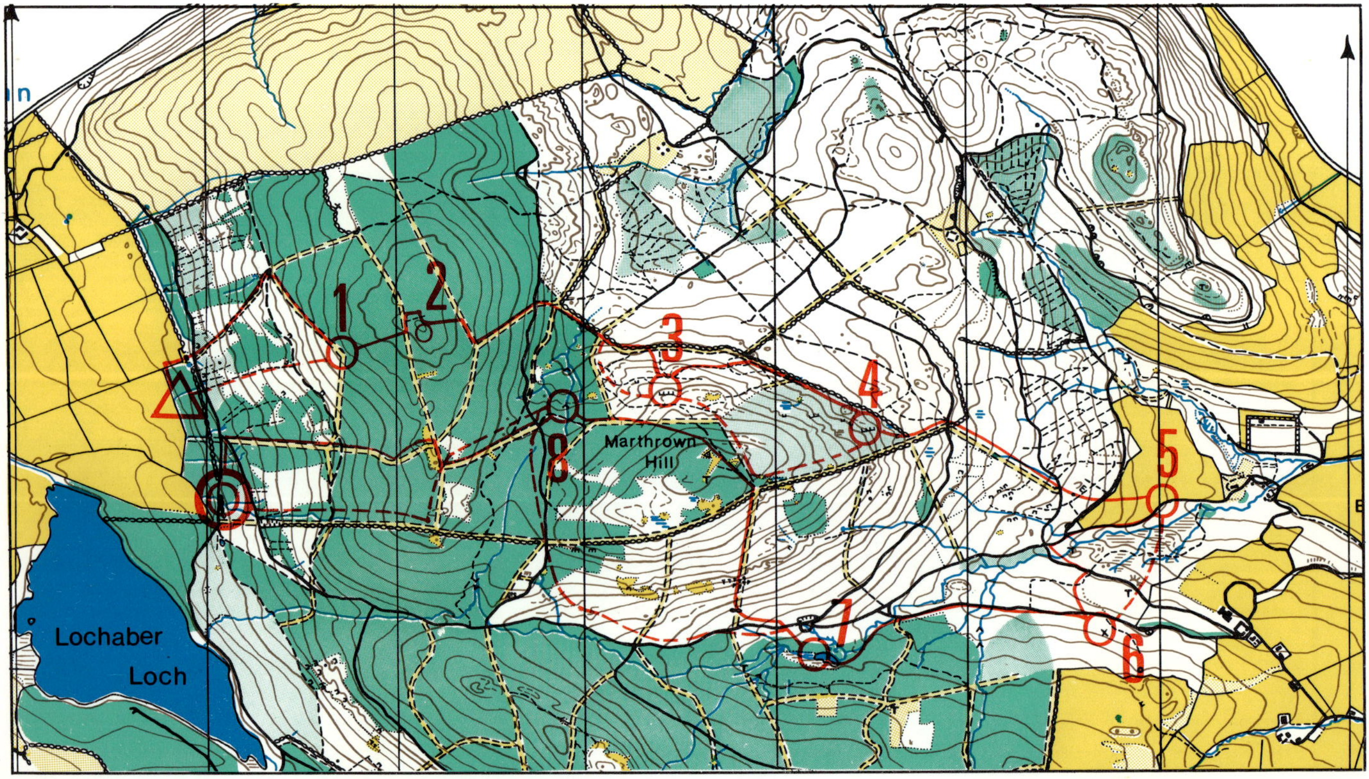

Linda - - - - -
Laura ———

Hallyburton Forest

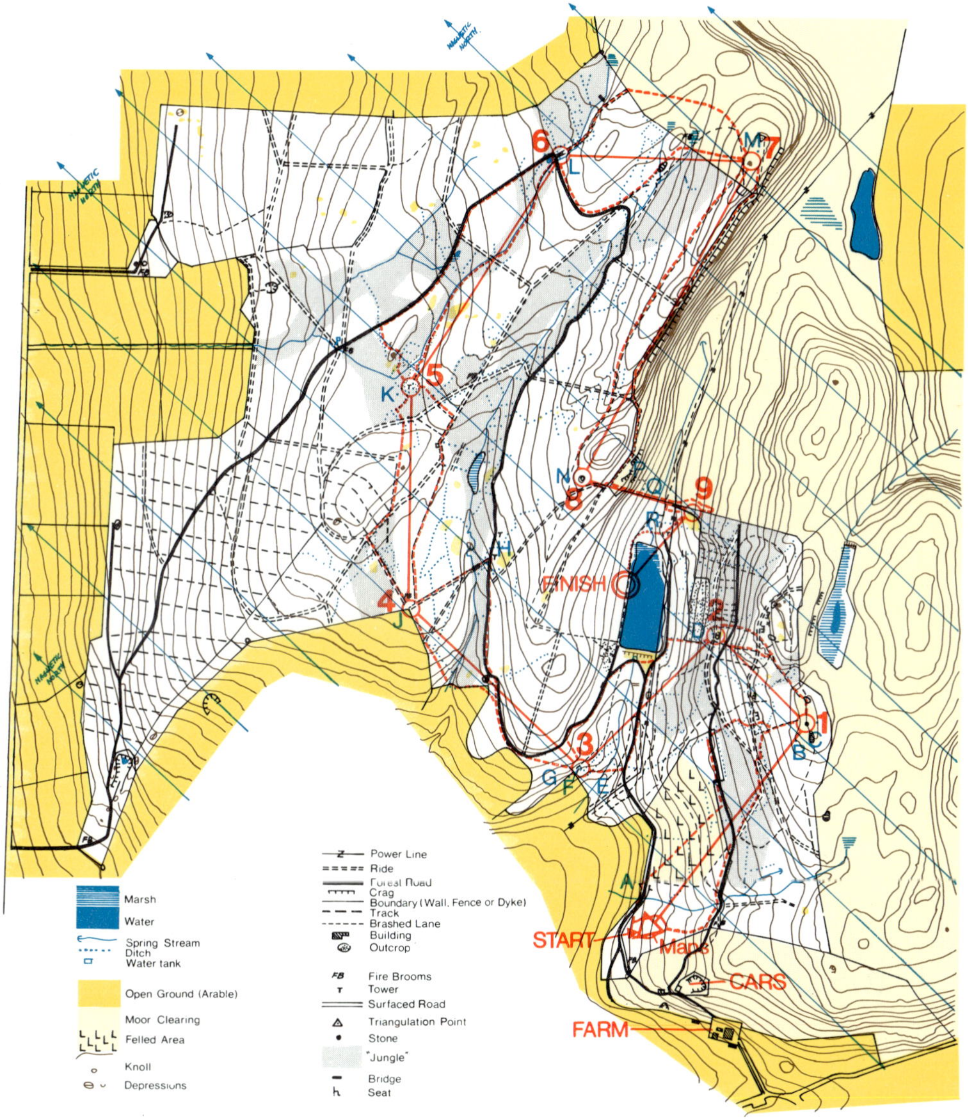

All other symbols are IOF

Letters indicate positions of photos.
Dotted red lines show two possible routes.